UNLIMITED HUMAN POTENTIAL:

A New Definition

Dr. John S. Morgan

*Looking within to discover your own
Unlimited Human Potential and
recognizing it in others to create
a more fulfilling life.*

UNLIMITED HUMAN POTENTIAL: A NEW DEFINITION
John S. Morgan

Library of Congress Cataloging-in-Publication Data

Morgan, John S.,
    Unlimited human potential : a new definition / John S. Morgan.
      p.   cm.
    Includes bibliographical references and index.
    ISBN 1-56825-019-3 : $14.95
    1. Self-actualization (Psychology)   2. Success—Psychological
aspects.   I. Title.
BF637.S4M65   1994   94-7645
158'.1—dc20   CIP

Printed in the United States of America

Design and Typesetting: Publishing Professionals, New Port Richey, FL.
Cover Design: Tracy Hall
Production Coordinator: Barbara Hagen
Printing and Binding: Walsworth Publishing Co.

Dedication

To my Mother for the love, acceptance and compassion she has given me.

To Meredith for the love, acceptance and compassion we share.

To David John in the hope that the world he grows up in is full of love, acceptance and compassion.

Contents

Acknowledgment

I met Louise Thompson three years ago when a friend referred me to her for advice. Louise owns a marketing and public relations agency, and I wanted help developing and marketing business/motivational seminars. I wanted to start out doing them in the Tampa Bay area and to eventually take them national.

While Louise liked my thoughts and ideas, she told me that success in conducting seminars on a national scale came primarily to those who authored books. She advised me to write one. Me? Write a book? Who is she kidding? I thought. What would I say?

Louise, I discovered later, is a freelance journalist and author. She offered to help me write a book.

When I left her ninth floor offices overlooking Tampa Bay, I had an assignment in hand. Louise gave me a single sheet of yellow-lined legal paper on which she had written in thick black marker across the top: What I Want to Tell the World and Why?

"Go home, John," she had told me, "and look at this whenever you have a free moment." "You'll know what to do."

Louise Thompson's belief in me, in my ideas and my ability to respond to her assignment—and the questions she continually posed—is the story behind the story of *UNLIMITED HUMAN POTENTIAL: A New Definition*. Three months after our first meeting, I mailed her 50 pages of manuscript. We met for breakfast after she had read them. We talked. I mailed her more. We met again. And on and on we went for over two years, meeting every three or four months in the beginning, and every few weeks as I finished writing down my thoughts and beliefs, my philosophies and ideas.

Louise took what I had written and edited it in a way that made it all understandable and easy to read. To do this, she literally got inside my head as she worked on and edited

ix

UNLIMITED HUMAN POTENTIAL: A New Definition. She is as much a believer in the concepts of love, acceptance and compassion as I am.

Simply put, this book would not have been started without Louise Thompson. It would not have been written without Louise Thompson, and it would not have been completed without Louise Thompson.

I thank her for believing in me. For her craft and talent in writing and editing. For the help she's been to me by asking and helping me answer those bold black words on that yellow sheet of paper.

Preface

"The mind is like a parachute, it only works when it's open."
An anonymous inscription on a friend's poster.

In the movie *Dead Poet's Society*, actor Robin Williams is English professor John Keating, a teacher serving up non-traditional lessons. His students are young men from wealthy families with no time for parenting. In exchange for large sums of money, the students' parents expect the boarding school's all-male faculty to teach their progeny tradition in an atmosphere of stern discipline and moral propriety.

Professor Keating is on a different kind of mission, one which encourages independent thinking, decision-making that comes from questioning society's beliefs and authority's unwritten rules. Keating wants his students to attend to and trust their own feelings, to identify and stand up for their own convictions, to become everything that they can become. This English teacher wants his kids to know and to live lives filled with passion—not passivity.

In one scene, Keating jumps on his desk to demonstrate looking at life from a non-traditional perspective. He encourages his students—some more reluctant to break with the rules than others—to follow his lead. If we look at people and events in the same old way, nothing will change, he tells us. If we experience life from only one vantage point, we impose limitations on our line of sight. We won't, Keating teaches us, be in a position to understand and accept anyone or anything that falls outside of our field of vision if we sit, every day of our lives, at our old familiar desks.

Risking a look at life from a different perspective doesn't mean we will decide to stay atop someone else's desk. It doesn't mean we'll alter our views enormously. After all, we know we can jump off and return to our original seats.

But, once we've explored life from a new angle, we've broadened our outlook and ourselves. We've come to realize that we each have a desk that is uniquely our own and that everyone else has a desk that is uniquely his or her own. Looking at life from another vantage point is the first step we take in learning to understand and accept other people and their beliefs. It's the first step we take in learning to understand and accept the behaviors of others. Behaviors that are unlike our own and, oftentimes, that we find difficult to comprehend.

Acknowledging that we all have our own desk and our own perspective is just a single step. But, nothing we do after we have sat for a while at someone else's desk will ever be the same.

I have written this book as an invitation to you. An invitation to look at life from my desk. My invitation is not unlike the one Professor Keating extended in *Dead Poet's Society* when he asked his students to come to the front of their classroom and to stand atop his desk. To look at the old wooden desks and wide black chalkboard from an unfamiliar point of view.

I want very much to share with you some ideas I have been collecting over the past several years. So that it won't get in your way, I invite you to leave your own desk behind. Temporarily, that is. Come with me for a little while and have a look at the view from where I sit.

Getting Started

Interpreting the World

*H*uman beings have been making efforts to interpret the world they live in forever. Anthropologists' treasures—slabs of stone and other long-buried artifacts—affirm that prehistoric beings were intrigued with life around them. Through primitive drawings and symbols, we know they wished to communicate with others what was happening for them.

Pictures drawn on cave walls—hieroglyphics—reflect people's views of life as they experienced it physically. Scenes depict hunting, fishing, preparing food, caring for the young. None, I believe, express thoughts about personal growth and human development. We have no evidence that self-help cave walls existed. That there was an audience for drawings designed to help others with self-esteem problems, identity crises, dysfunctionalities and so on.

In those days, everyone's goal was simply to stay alive. Quality of life issues, inner peace and happiness issues, were not uppermost on their minds or in their communications.

15

The Search for Quality in Our Lives

*F*or primitive men and women, staying alive was paramount. It is still an important drive and ambition. But the need for quality in our lives has emerged as vital to our well being.

Thousands of books have been published in the last century or so on improving our quality of life. Some are quite specific, while others speak to changes in our overall philosophy of life.

We can buy advice on choosing careers, acquiring and handling money, increasing our state of physical fitness, changing our diets, developing our cooking skills and learning more about technology and computers. We can buy books to increase our knowledge in any given area. We can be better-informed hobbyists, speakers, writers and gardeners.

These books deal with who, what, where, how and when situations.

Personal growth and self-help books, the numbers of which have skyrocketed in the last decade, suggest that if we develop personally—inside—then all other aspects of our lives will be enhanced.

These books deal with why.◻

Reading Poetry

I remember reading difficult poetry in junior high and high school, rhyming verses that I knew had profound meaning, but that I just didn't get. No matter how hard I tried—how many words I looked up in my dictionary or how many times I re-read one of these poems—I sometimes could not understand what the author wished to convey.

But then, suddenly, after a teacher, one of my parents or another student made some comment about the poem, I would begin understanding it. I would get from the way others strung their ideas or thoughts together about a poem some idea that created meaning for me. A light, as they say, would go on in my head.

My interpretation of a piece of poetry turned out sometimes to be quite different from the interpretations my classmates had. Theirs from one another. Ours from our teacher's.

That didn't matter. That was okay. What was important, I think, was that the poem finally made some sense to me. That I understood. That gave me the confidence I needed to try interpreting another poem. And another.

What you're about to read is, I suppose, my interpretation of the poetry called life. It's probably different from other author's interpretations. From my junior high school English teacher's interpretation. From your interpretation. And, that's okay. It's fine. I just want to share it with you.➤

The Wheel of Life

Society's Graph

*S*ociety seems to characterize us according to a set of accomplishments that we can graph.

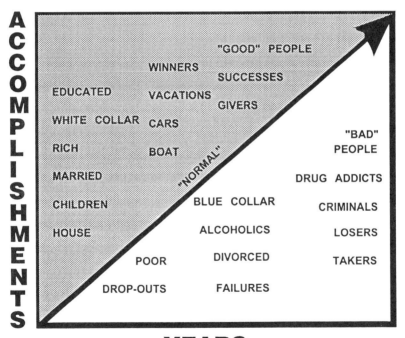

We begin our journeys as newborns who learn, at different stages, to sit up, crawl, walk and run. We are exposed to parents, family and others and we become more knowledgable as we accumulate information from our surroundings. We attend school and college, take a number of jobs, earn more and more money. We marry, have kids and, society assumes, become happier and happier. This is how we "should" progress—how we will move "up" the graph. But, our culture recognizes that some of us don't always achieve in this way. That some of us even move "down" the graph.

Some of us drop out of school, settle for "bad" jobs, become criminals, get divorced, file for bankruptcy and deal with a host of other "problems." Society accepts that this happens and points out that there are some of us who are low on the accomplishment graph. Some, who, as one radio talk show host labels us, are referred to as "bottom feeders."

It's as if an imaginary dotted line separated people as being winners or losers, rich or poor, happy or unhappy, successful or unsuccessful. Some of us on both ends of the graph are upset, angry and disgusted at those on the other end of the graph. But, we all accept, somehow, our particular position on the graph.

Those of us who are on the top of the dotted line generally believe that people get where they are going by making choices. If those choices are "bad" or "poor," individuals and groups suffer consequences that move them down the graph. If those choices are "good" or "appropriate," people reap benefits and move up the graph. This is how we justify our being on the top of the dotted line and how we justify that others are on the bottom of the dotted line.

Those of us who are on the bottom of the dotted line, on the other hand, generally believe that "good" luck, circumstance and fate put some of us on the top of the dotted line and that "bad" luck, circumstance and fate put others of us on the bottom of the dotted line. We can, in this way, rationalize where we are.

Books are written and sold to teach us how to make choices that will help us become successes or winners. That will help us move up the graph and onto the top of the dotted line. They tell us about choices that will deliver to us an abundance of happiness, fulfillment and prosperity. The most popular books are directed at those individuals who occupy positions under the imaginary dotted line. Many of these books tell stories of people who beat the odds and their dysfunctionalities, to use a popular term, to rise to a life of fame, fortune and/or fulfillment. These are interesting and entertaining stories. Some are valuable. But, all seem to perpetuate society's beliefs that there exists only winners and losers, successes and failures.

I don't agree with this way of thinking. What it does is value some people and devalue others.❖

Value One Another

I would throw out the graph and replace it with a wheel where everyone begins life in the center.

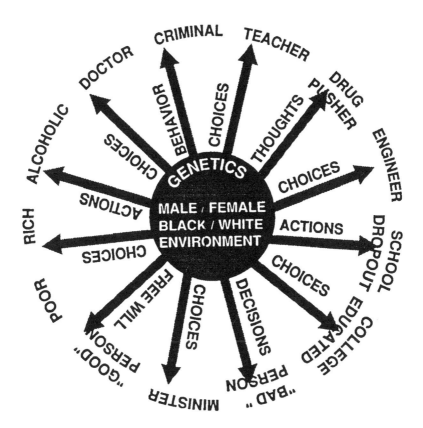

Choices we make take us out toward a range of different spokes to some particular place on the wheel's rim. One side of the wheel is no "better" than another side. There is no "good,"

"bad," "right" or "wrong." No bottom. And, no top. All the locations on the wheel's rim are exactly the same distance from the wheel's center.

The concept of life as a wheel is not confining, not static as is the concept of life as a graph. Viewing all of us as on a wheel encourages motion without valuing—devaluing particular choices. Choices are continuously being made and positions are constantly being changed.

At any given moment, we are somewhere on the wheel's rim, our position determined by the choices we decide to make.☯

Free Will and Choices

*E*veryone has free will and everyone makes choices. Our choices are made based on our present level of awareness. These choices are not "bad" or "good." They are not "right" or "wrong." Since each of us is unique, our choices, however, are simply "unique."

No two of us, then, can ever occupy an identical position on life's wheel. We may, indeed, be in similar positions, but we may never be in locations which are exactly alike. The number of possible positions we can choose to occupy is infinite.

No matter what choices we make, no matter what the consequences, all of us are on the rim of the wheel. *We are all equal in value—equal as human beings.*

Choices made by individuals who have known nothing but war and/or hunger will be different from choices made by others. Choices made by people who come from different countries, cultures, economies and ethics will also be different.

People who appear to share similar circumstances or experiences may make choices totally opposite of each other.

One 18-year-old may decide to drop out of school and rob banks; another may choose to go to college and study engineering. Some of our choices may enhance our lives; others may contribute to destroying them. Free will and choice are complex issues going beyond socioeconomic status and the expectations we make.

Awareness

No Failure, Only Awareness

M ost people fail miserably when it comes to understanding themselves and the world around them.

I used the word "fail" purposely. You see, in , there is no failure. It may be true that you and I have a difficult time understanding ourselves and those around us. But, this does not represent failure. It represents our level of awareness. *Our ability to understand, to change, to transform ourselves, is based solely, I believe, on our present level of awareness and not on any notion of failure.*

Awareness may make it hard for us to view the world as a wheel, for example, or to see ourselves out on a wheel's rim occupying some invisible position.

I know, as you do, more after reading a few pages of a book than I did moments before I opened it. As our knowledge expands to include other's thoughts and ideas our awareness broadens. Our thinking and our actions may change from whatever enlightenment we have from increased knowledge. But, it may not. After all, everyone is different. Everyone's awareness level is uniquely his or her own. Our ability to understand and to transform ourselves is also quite unique.

The key, I think, is to become more aware of our awareness.

This is where I am right now. My thoughts and actions are not always what I would like them to be. But, at this moment, I am aware of those thoughts and actions. I am, then, somewhat aware of my present level of awareness.

As we become aware of our unique awareness, transformation occurs. Change may or may not be rapid, but the process is without doubt a gloriously dynamic one.➤

Awareness of Our Awareness

*F*or a moment, allow yourself to be where you are right now. Accept that you have a position on the wheel's rim. Become aware of where that is.

When we allow ourselves to just be where we are, to accept our own position on the wheel's rim, we simultaneously allow others to be themselves. We accept them more easily. We understand their uniqueness, their positions on the rim.

Here's one way we can learn more about ourselves. When we meet someone new, we can tune into our thoughts and feelings. What is generated when we think about a new business acquaintance or prospective client or customer? How do we feel meeting a member of the opposite sex at a social gathering? What's happening in our minds when we chat with a friend or a friend of a partner? Someone new to us? Or, someone we've known a while? What are we thinking when someone passes us on the street?

To become aware of our thoughts and feelings, we can look at the questions we may be asking ourselves.

I wonder what she/he is thinking about me?
Is she/he like me?
It looks like she/he has gained weight.
She/he looks successful.
She/he looks like a loser.
Am I attracted to him/her?
She/he seems nice.
I think I could like this person.
I think I would have a difficult time liking this person.

There are no "wrong" thoughts or feelings. Some questions or thoughts might appear inappropriate or judgmental or prejudicial. This doesn't matter. What does matter is becoming aware of what we are thinking or feeling, period. As we do this, we may determine the thoughts we have which lead to understanding and accepting others. We may also begin to recognize feelings that lead to confusion.

At some point, we begin to recognize those thoughts and questions we have that come from acceptance and those that come from our prejudices. As we give ourselves permission to have the feelings we have, we allow ourselves to ask questions. Down the road, this process may result in change. Change that brings us great rewards. ❖

A Hard Time

*F*or several years, I have met twice weekly with ten to twelve friends. Between 6 A.M. and 7 A.M. we play basketball at a local sports facility. Afterwards, we have breakfast and talk about a variety of subjects, some of which do not include our potential for NBA first-round draft picks.

We give each other a "hard time" regularly. We do this for fun and no one seems offended including whoever becomes the recipient of the hard time.

I've become aware of what is being said at these sessions. That is, I am attending more closely with what is being said by the others and with what I am saying.

While I'm sure that most of our comments are not meant to hurt or degrade anyone, they certainly are conveyed in that context. I find it difficult to determine whether some of our remarks are harmless or if they are destructive.

Please understand that I am not judging, interpreting or perceiving these gatherings or my friends. I am just becoming aware of them.

I am interested and aware of my friends, you can be sure. But, I am becoming more aware of my own role, my own participation, in these breakfast breaks.

At one time—not long ago —I did not give my comments a second thought.

But, now, as I become increasingly aware of myself and my words, I see that my role and my participation in these sessions are changing somewhat.

Does this mean that my comments are now completely loving, accepting and compassionate? Of course not. I continue making some of the same comments I did before tuning into them. It's just that I am now aware of what I am saying. I am also aware of feeling differently when I say something that does not reflect my true nature. Comments that are not loving, accepting and compassionate. ↬

He's Not a Loser

*O*n one particular morning, one of the guys with whom I play basketball talked about his wife. He told us that she was extraordinarily competitive. She loved winning so much, he said, that she would do anything and everything to achieve her goals.

I said, "That's probably because she married such a big loser." Everyone laughed, including my friend.

He's not a loser, of course. He is physically, financially and emotionally secure. He has high self-esteem. I don't know anyone who doesn't respect and admire him. This may have been why everyone laughed. The remark was so off-base.

As the others laughed I became aware of what I had said. And, I became aware of what I felt. The comment I made was not constructive. None of my friends probably gave it a second thought. In fact, they probably had forgotten it before we finished our last cups of coffee.

But, I still feel the feeling I had then. It's not a feeling of guilt. Not a "bad" feeling.

It's a feeling I get when my behavior doesn't reflect my true nature.

I do welcome this feeling because it allows me to become more aware. That awareness and the thoughts produced by that awareness allow me to feel differently than I did before. Feelings, we know, are what drives our behavior. So, feeling as I did after my comment, helps me come closer to my true nature.

I believe that as we become aware of our unlimited human potential, our thoughts change. When our thoughts change, our feelings change. When our feelings change, our behavior changes.

Our whole being—our whole existence—becomes more loving, accepting and compassionate. ☯

Unlimited Human Potential

It's in All of Us—Equally

*U*nlimited—I mean absolutely boundless—human potential resides in each of us. It is manifested in our feelings of love, acceptance and compassion.

As our awareness increases, our being is transformed. We think less. We become, as Dr. Deepak Chopra suggests, "silent witnesses." We get to a place where we can "just be there" in the present with other beings.

When we are transformed, we cease to evaluate, to interpret, to categorize, to label and to judge. Thoughts of love, acceptance and compassion become unnecessary. Our whole being becomes love, acceptance and compassion.

We transcend our "self." We become one with others.◻

Words

God	Cause
God within	It
Spirit	True nature
Consciousness	True self
Infinite power	Higher self
Universal mind or thought	The thing

*L*ike most people, I have favorite words. Words I use over and over again. Unlimited human potential, for example, is a phrase I use throughout this book.

These three words mean a lot to me. You may be as comfortable with them as I am or you may not. They are not exclusive words. There are other words that you may use to express what you feel.

Use God within, infinite power, higher-self or any other words with which you are more at ease. Individuals who read my manuscript before it was published represent various belief systems and religions. Some red-lined the phrase "unlimited human potential" and replaced it with one or more words which spoke greater clarity to them. This was a great idea. Please do the same if you have words that better describe what you feel.

I also use the words love, acceptance and compassion to represent our humanness. These words are my expression of being or arriving at unlimited human potential. Unlimited human potential is something you are. And that something allows you to be all that is loving, accepting and compassionate.

Choose different words if you like. The synonym lists in a Thesaurus are long ones.

The point is that the words I like are just that: words I like. They are not right or wrong, good or bad. You have the freedom to pick and choose your own words and phrases. The ones which speak to you and your own truth.➤

Unlimited Human Potential—A Definition

Unlimited means having no limits. It means having no bounds, having no qualifications.

Potential is defined as capable of being—not yet in existence. To have potential, then, one must be capable.

During the Olympics, event commentators use phrases like, "She/he has the ability to win" and "She/he is capable of breaking the world record." These phrases are not used in the descriptions of ALL Olympic participants. Some, as talented as they may be, are viewed as incapable of winning. They were not judged as having the ability to break an event's world record. They lacked potential—because they did not possess some necessary capabilities.

According to this definition, to have potential, one must be capable. But this suggests a limitation on potential.

Each one of us is capable of doing things. Most are capable of sleeping, eating, walking, smiling, etc. We are also capable of taking risks, loving people, working at new jobs, excelling in a particular sport, etc.

When there is capability, there is, without doubt, potentiality. But, we probably all agree, that we must be capable at something to have the potential to achieve in that area.

Michael Jordan and Larry Byrd, incredibly talented basketball players were, for as long as they were members of National Basketball Association (NBA) teams, capable and, consequently, had the potential to win NBA championships.

You and I aren't capable of winning an NBA championship. We don't have that potential.

45

Putting the word "unlimited" before the word "potential" tosses out the limiting aspects of this definition of "potential." It tosses out the need for "capabilities," as we use them to describe Olympic athletes, professional basketball players and others. The definition of potential is broadened. It becomes "being"—not CAPABLE of being. It becomes "being, not yet in existence."

By putting "unlimited" ahead of the word "potential" we void out any need for capability.

Having unlimited potential means we don't reach something. We don't get something. We don't achieve something. Having unlimited potential is existing in an unlimited state of being.

Inserting the word *"human"* between the words "unlimited" and "potential" tells us that as human beings what we have is unlimited human potential.

I'm not talking about unlimited "you-can-do-whatever-you-want-to-do" potential. I'm not talking about unlimited "get-a-better-job" potential. Nor about unlimited "financial" potential or unlimited "athletic" potential or unlimited "you-fill-in-the-blank" potential.

There is a world of difference between those descriptions of unlimited potential and mine.

I want you to know about unlimited "human" potential.

What do I mean? What are the qualities that make us human? What is the true nature of being human?

To be human, I believe, is to be loving, accepting and compassionate.

All of us know what it is to be loving, accepting and compassionate. We all display these qualities of humanness sometimes. But, at other times, we also exhibit what we might call "opposite" kinds of qualities. No matter who we are, where we are on life's wheel, we all exhibit these different kinds of human qualities.

Our true nature, I believe, is to be loving, accepting and compassionate. This may be difficult to accept. It may be even more difficult to accept that the true nature of others we know or hear or read about is to be loving, accepting and compassionate. But it is so.

We are, I know, capable of being hateful, selfish and judgmental. We can be consumed with fear, anger and prejudice. To be these things, though, to display these emotions, is not our true nature.

I think when our behaviors and thoughts conflict with our true nature, we suffer confusion. This confusion may be conscious, but, usually it is unconscious.

As we become more aware of ourselves, our thoughts and our behaviors, we discover more of our unlimited human potential. Our confusion dissipates as our thoughts and our behaviors become congruent with our true nature, which is to be loving, accepting and compassionate.

We have the potential to become more loving, accepting and compassionate every day. To bring into everything we do more love, acceptance and compassion. This is our true nature as humans.❖

Life Just Is

*U*nlimited human potential is synonymous with life or life force.

And that begs the question: What is life? What is that state of being that tells us when something is alive?

Unlimited human potential, I believe, is born when sperm unites with an egg. No one truly understands this yet and no one can truly explain it.

We can agree, though, that life is. That unlimited human potential just is.❂

Acceptance Without Proof

*H*ave you ever thought about what actually happens when someone cuts his or her arm? After the bleeding stops and time has passed, the cut is gone. How does this happen? Theories have been developed to explain the physical healing that takes place between wound and wellness. But, theories are only scientific guesses. No more. No less.

We cannot with certainty explain the healing of a cut. We cannot explain life or life force either. Some—many, in fact—call unlimited human potential God. Others use different explanations. What we name life force—our labels for life force—are not truly relevant. What is important is acknowledging that life and unlimited human potential just are.

If we make a cut into the arm of someone who has been in a coma for five years, we will see the cut heal. If we make a cut into the arm of someone who recently died, the cut will not heal. The dead person's body can be seen. His or her life, his or her own unlimited human potential—however, is gone.

Right?☐

Nurturing Our Beings

*I*n the movie *Awakenings*, a factual film, we learned about a group of middle-aged men and women who had contracted encephalitis at an early age. The illness caused these gentle beings to become catatonic, a state which rendered their arms and legs stiff and immovable. This caused them to appear emotionally and physically unresponsive to anything or anyone. As the movie depicted, these men and women were for all intents and purposes "asleep."

For 30 years they were hospitalized along with individuals who suffered from chronic and serious mental illnesses.

The encephalitis victims were treated as if they were not alive on the inside. Regarded by many of the hospital's staff and administrators as objects, the patients were bathed, dressed, fed, moved from beds to community rooms and back again, examined and drugged. But, they were not accorded much of what we know as human kindness. Not extended the same caring gestures that others of us take for granted.

In the summer of 1969, a young, newly-hired doctor, curious about his charges, studied their charts and histories, talked to their families, investigated their automatic responses. He theorized that this group of encephalitis victims were alive, and that they had the potential to express that aliveness.

He believed, without proof, that their life force was locked up inside of them and that a key was needed to open the doorway to its freedom. To its expression.

The researcher-turned-physician persuaded hospital higher-ups to allow him to administer to these patients a drug called L-Dopa—a then-new medicine being used in the treatment of Parkinson's Disease.

Shortly, a miracle happened. The life force of these patients awakened. The men and women began talking. Moving their arms and legs. Feeling emotions. They laughed, smiled, became sad, cried. They were angry and they were elated.

Had they—before taking L-Dopa—been totally absent any life force? Was life created by L-Dopa? Had it always been there, but untapped and uninspired?

I believe their unlimited human potential, life, life force, God, whatever, was always there but just not in a way that any of us could understand.

For the stars of *Awakenings*, their story ended sadly. Their arousal from sleep did not last. Within a short period of time, they returned to their catatonia. L-Dopa's usefulness appeared temporary.

More permanent, however, was the change that occurred in those who attended to this group. Aware that their unlimited human potential did indeed exist, their caregivers treated them differently. They read to them, talked with them, joked with them, touched them. They bestowed on them what we all need to nourish and to nurture our life force, the God within us, our unlimited human potential.➤

Healing and Science

$\mathcal{T}$he best healers in the world are those who understand—who accept—that unlimited human potential resides in all people.

We don't need a medical degree to accept this notion. In some ways, the education involved in obtaining a medical degree may impose limits on our acceptance of life force and God and unlimited human potential. For these ideas are not measurable or explainable. They cannot be rationalized. They are not scientific. Yet.

This is fine. I accept this. Science and scientists, I know, are needed. But, when it comes to healing, I believe that acknowledging unlimited human potential is not just essential. It is paramount.❖

Meredith's Kids

*M*y wife Meredith is a pediatric occupational therapist. She works with babies and young children who are not developing as they should because of a variety of problems. Some were traumatized during birth. Others came into the world with genetic abnormalities. Their development, it is known, lags behind other children of the same ages.

As Meredith works to help the children roll over, crawl, stand, walk, learn, feed and care for themselves, she carries with her the beliefs of a true healer. These children have unlimited human potential, she knows that. They are not objects—no matter their level of development. They are unlimited human beings housed in bodies different than others who represent our society's majority.

Meredith uses love and compassion, kindness and touch to help her charges reach new steps on their journeys. The responses she receives are quite different than those received by others who excel in the mechanical aspects of occupational therapy—others who lack awareness about unlimited human potential and the way to nurture it. ☯

Orville's Gift

*I*n the summer of 1976, after completing my senior year at the University of Kansas, I trained for a try-out with the New York Jets and I met Orville. Since I was young boy, my life's goal had been to play college football. When the opportunity came to snap to Joe Namath, I couldn't pass it up. Besides, playing professional football had more appeal to me than work on an advanced degree.

I met Orville while visiting my grandfather in a Milwaukee nursing home over summer break. Sloppy and unshaven, Orville made a very different impression than did my properly-attired, impeccably well-groomed grandfather.

Orville took all his meals in the nursing room common area where he could observe all who visited. While he watched a baseball game on TV, I felt compelled to introduce myself. We liked each other instantly and, thereafter, I made it a point to chat with him whenever I visited my grandfather.

Orville had no family or friends. No one visited him. He had never been married and had no children. He was also ornery.

In the fall of 1976, when my brief career with the New York Jets had ended, I returned to college. I never wrote to Orville while I lived away from home, but I visited him on school breaks and holidays. My grandfather passed away in 1978, but I continued visiting Orville at the nursing home and our friendship grew.

Orville experienced a decline in his health as he grew older. On my visits back to Milwaukee while away at college, I made it a point to see him frequently. He slowly began losing weight. While retaining his mental abilities, Orville became increasingly lethargic and abnormally—for him—complacent. My friend was dying.

During my earlier visits, I watched his eyes twinkle and a gentle smile spread across his lips when I entered his room and stood before him. As time went on, though, his reactions to my presence faded. We talked less and less. He slept more. His brightness dimmed.

The outline of his body under his bed sheets became smaller as his weight decreased. Eventually, Orville lost consciousness. My visits grew longer and more frequent as I became aware that he would pass away soon.

On a number of occasions, I took his warm hand into mine. Clasping it gently, I told him how much I loved him and how important our relationship was to me. While he was not conscious during our many talks, I am sure he felt my presence.

Those final visits with Orville were some of the most precious times of my life. What I did not know then, but am sure of now, is that I was communicating with Orville's unlimited human potential. Indeed, it was my unlimited human potential that had communed with his unlimited human potential.

I know this because I felt complete love, acceptance and compassion while I sat with Orville. For brief moments in time, I felt the ecstasy that was the unity of our beings.

Orville passed away peacefully. His body does not grace this earth. It died. But, the unlimited human potential, God, infinite mind, universal power that was my friend Orville did not pass away. It never will. Orville lives through me and, as I come in contact with you, through you.□

Love and Potential

We each have something of great value to offer. We've each seen evidence of our enormous potential to give something of ourselves that touches and gladdens the heart of someone else. Haven't we all been incredibly kind at some point or another? Haven't we all been enormously uplifting to someone sometime? Don't we all remember helping a friend or a stranger feel less isolated? more understood? Isn't this potential in us worth releasing more fully? Releasing and spreading. If what we think we are today isn't calling to us for greater consistency in what we can give, then, surely, what we think we could be is. Our potential is love and love is of God. To help others become happier will do more for us than increase our own happiness. It will release the world from pain. Turn hell into heaven for every living thing. Our potential as healers has no boundary beyond which it cannot go.

Paraphrased from Hugh Prather

Isn't it wonderful to know that all of us have this potential? To know that even those of us who don't know it have it?

Our task isn't to let others know this; our task is to live our own potential.➤

Transformation

Asking

*W*hen I was a young child I asked my mother, "Where is God?"

She answered, "Everywhere."

"Not just in heaven?" I asked.

"No," she said, "God is everywhere."

"But, I can't see Him," I told her. "Is He in front of my face?"

"Yes," she said, "God is everywhere and God is everything."

"Is He in this cup of Kool-Aid?" I asked. "This house? My dog Molly?"

"Well, Johnny, I guess so," she said. "Yes, yes, God is everywhere and everything. He is even inside of you."

"Okay," I said, finally. "God is everywhere, everything and inside of me. Right?"

"There you go," she said. "Now, you have it."

This is one of those things I was taught and I accepted. If I had considered it too much, I probably would have gone crazy. So, I just grew up with the notion that God was everything and everywhere. And, God, I knew, was inside of me.

This was much like the time my Dad told me there were more stars in the sky than there were grains of sand on an enormous beach. That notion seemed hard to comprehend, but I just believed it anyway. I did not, after all, have time to dwell on these ideas and issues. There were waves to ride, footballs to toss and baseballs to bat. I was a kid and I was most interested in having fun.

All of us, I suppose, contemplate that which is not easily explained. We think about the unknowns, the mysterious, where we come from and why we are here. We wonder whether there is a God, what came before us, if there is life after death.

Some of us ask profound questions when we are youngsters and then just forget about them because it is more simple to accept our parents' explanations. The answers, we instinctively know, are hard to come by. Some of us search our whole lives for answers to life's big questions. Others of us wait until we are close to death to ponder these things.

I'm one of those people who stopped asking questions, stopped thinking about them when I was a young child, but who began wondering about them again some years later.

My life is not consumed with finding the answers. I am not obsessed with having to "know." I do, however, enjoy enormously the process, the pursuit of answers. A trip I once found confusing, frustrating and even frightening is now exciting, fascinating and incredibly calming.

The types of questions we all ask and the possible answers to them fill libraries and book stores all over our world. It isn't my intent to argue or to agree with any of them. I just happen to have my own ideas.❖

Self-Actualization

*O*ver the past year, my life has changed rather dramatically. An ongoing process, no doubt and one that will continue for the rest of my years.

I still go to work every day. I play basketball, participate in triathalons, lift weights and do aerobics as I have for many years. I am in love with my wife Meredith and I enjoy the support and loyalty of a family I love. I have wonderful friends. I read a great deal and love learning, as I always have.

So what then has changed? Certainly nothing about my outside world and my involvement in it. What has been transforming is my inner world. I am in the process of discovering my own unlimited human potential.

I have, for some time, read books, attended seminars and listened to audio cassettes devoted to the broad topic of unlimited human potential. I thought all of my learnings on this topic had to do with getting a better job, making more money, becoming increasingly successful in a material sense.

It was once clear to me that if I had a plan—a detailed step-by-step, five-year strategy—and if I took the appropriate daily actions and if I unfailingly persisted, I would achieve and accomplish anything I desired because of something called unlimited human potential.

I figured, in other words, if I do, do, do, I will get, get, get.

I also thought that it was essential to recognize and maximize my unlimited human potential. To pursue this course to achieve and accomplish some tangible, defined goals. While I do continue to believe that we are—each one of us—capable of accomplishing great feats, my personal concept of what is unlimited human potential has changed.

It isn't do, do, do to get, get, get. Unlimited human potential is about realization. About awareness. A famed psychologist, Dr. Abraham Maslow, long ago introduced a concept called self-actualization. It ranked top place on human beings' hierarchy of needs. Self-actualization has to do with a realization and an awareness that inside each one of us there exists an unlimited human being. One who has unlimited human potential.

Self-actualization is, I believe, self-realization and self-awareness. It is not, make no mistake about it, my realization that you or anyone else is unlimited. It IS my realization that I am unlimited. It is YOUR own realization that YOU are unlimited.☯

Look Inside

$\mathcal{T}$he 1980's was a decade of tremendous economic growth for many. More people, it has been reported, became millionaires in the 1980's than in all the other decades preceding it combined.

Prosperity consciousness marked our last decade. It was okay—good even—to make money. The amassing of wealth was not considered, as it might have been in the past, an evil pursuit. It was rationalized, in fact, that the more money we accumulated, the more we could and would do for society.

Our collective goal, then, was to make as much money as we possibly could. We would not be embarrassed with buying things. We were encouraged, in fact, to buy bigger homes, more luxurious automobiles, fancier boats and heavenly vacation timeshares.

But, in the 1980's, we also witnessed a rise in divorce, depression, drug abuse, criminality and suicide. Many of us who prospered financially found ourselves experiencing seriously difficult times in non-financial matters. No one was immune. The rich and the poor, the young and the old all had their share of problems. Most unfortunately, this pattern seems to be continuing into the 1990's.

Individuals continue striving for happiness and fulfillment by changing jobs, earning more money and connecting with new partners. I have to wonder, as you probably do, if it is working.

While we all hope and pray for a peaceful world without conflict, we know in our hearts, we won't see this anytime soon. The search for happiness and fulfillment outside of ourselves, it seems clear, is becoming an increasingly futile way to expend our energies.

I think we should look within—not outside ourselves—to find the happiness and fulfillment we so desire.◻

Inner Peace

*S*omething is still missing. We have accomplished our goals or we are working on them. Some of us are living more comfortably. We feel good about sharing what we have, about serving society in some way.

But, we are, as a whole, pretty unsettled. We are somehow uneasy with ourselves. We are, more simply, not happy.

We are missing, lacking inner peace. With our focus directed toward getting our outer worlds under control, we have neglected our inner worlds. And going to church weekly or monthly or volunteering a half-day here and there to help others hasn't solved the problem.

The answer, it seems, is not "out there."

Everything we could ever need, I firmly believe, we already have. We just need to look inside ourselves to discover it.

More of us are beginning this process of self-examination. Changes ARE coming. We want this illusive inner peace. We want happiness. And we will find them.

While the 1980's were a decade of "from-out-there" kinds of accumulation, accomplishment and achievement, the 1990's are fast becoming a decade of "in here" self-examination, self-awareness—a searching for inner peace. The 1990's will be the decade of personal transformation.➤

Selfishness

*I*n a world where there exists war, starvation, violence and homelessness—so much that needs our attention—how can we justify tending to ourselves? How can we turn away from our outer worlds to examine our inner selves? How can we think about inner peace with our universe in turmoil? Other people, after all, need us. Our planet needs us. If we spend time and expend energy becoming aware, what will happen to them?

Becoming selfish, concerning ourselves only with ourselves, is not what I am recommending. I don't believe we should—or that we can—divorce ourselves from life to go "find" ourselves. I am not saying that we can find ourselves by acting selfishly or by ignoring the people and the world around us.

But, I do want to stress that personal transformation and setting aside the necessary time for self-examination that this requires isn't, ultimately, a selfish act as many believe. As we develop from within, I believe our capacity to reach out and to touch others actually expands. We are enlarged.

Personal transformation is an unselfish pursuit. ❖

Deal With Your Own Personal Issues

*S*ome individuals concern themselves with saving and changing other people and the world. They want to perform this feat without taking the time and the energy to look at their own personal issues. Without self-examination. These people, I sometimes think, are as selfish—as detrimental to society perhaps—as those who ask for nothing and who give nothing.

I know they mean well. I know that, like most of us, they are doing the best that they possibly can do to make the world a better place.

But, let's look at our world's history. All negative impacts— war, racism, hunger, poverty—that have happened in our past, all indeed that is happening in our present, seem connected to someone's unresolved personal issues. Issues involving fear, guilt, blame and worry.

Rereading, rethinking our history from a new perspective just confirms that *destruction is the guaranteed result when one human being wants to control another.* When one human being wants to change another.

We see a negative impact every time one human being tries to "save" or control another human being. We see negative impacts every time groups of human beings decide they want, for their own selfish gain, to "save" or control another group of human beings. When people decide others ought to do things, believe things, in the same way they have chosen to do or believe things.

To heal our universe, we must—absolutely must—heal ourselves. First and Foremost. To fill our world with the love, the acceptance and the compassion we wish ourselves to enjoy, we must first love, accept and be compassionate with ourselves.

As we become aware of our inner selves, the world becomes aware. As we begin experiencing peace, our world begins feeling peace.

I have no doubt that as you and I become more loving, accepting and compassionate that personal issues will fade from our fields of vision. That, over time, we can—we will—eliminate fear, guilt, blame and worry. Every single one of those personal issues that result in war, racism, hunger, poverty and all that bring us and our fellow humans such great sadness and pain.

All of this can only happen if you and I begin the process of transformation by beginning to look inside of ourselves. If we look within ourselves and acknowledge our own Unlimited Human Potential—love, acceptance and compassion—wonderful changes will happen.

Our goal, however, is not change in itself. But rather it is in the *process* of changing.

We have, remember, learned many lessons from our pursuit of the material world. We learned that peace does not come from a larger house, more money or the accumulation of other goods. We learned that the process of doing brings us challenge, excitement, purpose, fun.

I do not expect people and the world to change.

I accept people and the world just the way they are.

I am in the process of changing myself. If, while I am in the process of changing myself, people and the world change, fine. Change in itself is unimportant. Change is not my goal.

Being involved in the process is everything.☯

Acknowledging Unlimited Human Potential

From Inside Out

*W*hen I began work on this book, I talked with my family and friends about it and about unlimited human potential. Most agreed the concept involved understanding our limitless possibilities, our capabilities to achieve and accomplish.

Both friends and families thought this was a natural topic for me because my life has been one filled with goal-setting and plans for accomplishing and achieving.

I have been, they are correct, externally motivated in many ways. I continue to be externally motivated. But, the unlimited human potential I am defining in my life, in this book, has become an internal concept. A strictly inside event.□

Potential is an Inside Event

*W*hile we grow, we often hear phrases like this: You're not working to your potential. You can do better than that. You have more potential than you are showing.

Most of us heard comments like these from parents, teachers, relatives, coaches and friends. Some of these phrases were used with regard to school work and athletics. Sometimes, the words were said to encourage us to practice our tubas, pianos, violins or guitars, to deal better with our brothers and sisters, mothers and fathers. To get us to clean our rooms or garages.

No matter who used comments like this or what they pertained to, many of us grew up thinking we could always do better than what we were doing. That we should or could do more.

We ask ourselves, "Why didn't I work up to my potential? How can I do better?"

When I talk about unlimited human potential, I am not sharing with you anything to do with increasing potential as it has to do with increasing our individual pools of money or our positions in some corporate hierarchy. Not about making straight A's or setting goals and devising plans to reach defined material gain. I am not talking about performing charitable acts, cleaning up the environment or any other very honorable deeds.

While doing any of those things is not "bad," I am not, for purposes of this book, interested in talking about them. They are externally motivated items that must be obtained, achieved or done.

I care about what is within.➤

Peel Back the Layers

I was born with unlimited human potential. I don't need to search outside myself to find it. I won't find it there. I must look within.

Unlimited human potential is an integral part of me, an integral part of you. At the core of our being, it resides. Awaiting our awareness. Awaiting our acknowledgment.

We came into the world with unlimited human potential. As babies, we were completely loving, accepting and compassionate. We were concerned with ourselves, perhaps, but this had nothing to do with selfishness. Babies, we know, are not selfish.

Where did our unlimited human potential go?

As a tree grows older, its initial core yields to a new layer. As each year passes, another layer is formed. Looking at a cross section of a cut tree trunk, we count the layers around its core to determine the tree's age. Each layer accounts for one year of growth. Twenty layers around the core, for example, tell us a tree is 20 years old.

We humans grow in layers just like trees do.

As we age, our true nature—our unlimited human potential—is covered up with a blend of genetic makeup and environmental experience. If it were possible to see our layers as we can see a tree's layers, we might find layer upon layer of hate, prejudice, judgment, jealousy, worry, fear, guilt, blame or other feelings we have learned or experienced.

Each one of us, I believe, possesses a number of these sorts of layers in different measures of thickness.

When we go looking for our unlimited human potential—our core—we need to look beyond—beneath—these layers. We acknowledge their existence. Yes. But, we determine to look beyond them.

This is possible for each of us no matter how many layers cover our inner core. No matter how thick each one may be.

If we want to find our unlimited human potential, we will find it. We may wish to peel back one layer at a time to accomplish this. Or, we may wish to use a giant ax to chop through several or all of them at once. It matters not the path. When we journey to our unlimited human potential, we find it. We need only desire to carry us through.❖

Just Be

*A*s we begin discovering our unlimited human potential, our view of ourselves and the world around us changes.

We arrive at different levels of understanding. Our journey—and our changes—may be calm and gradual. Or, they may be dramatic and rapid. Again, this doesn't matter. What does matter is that our awareness of our unlimited human potential increases. That our thoughts, feelings and behavior begin reflecting our inner core. A core composed entirely of love, acceptance and compassion.

We will experience times when our thoughts, feelings and behaviors are not congruent with our true nature. But, our awareness of these occasions expands. We are able to accept ourselves at all times. Even as we understand and become more alert to those thoughts, feelings and behaviors that do not seem loving, accepting and compassionate.

We allow ourselves to "just be." Not to judge. Not to interpret. Not to perceive. We simply become silent witnesses. And, as we do, our thoughts, feelings and behaviors become more aligned with our true nature, our inner core. We become love, acceptance and compassion, all that is our unlimited human potential. ❧

Words and the Feelings We Create

*W*hat words do we use describing how we feel hugging our partners, our children or other people we love. How do we explain our love for pets to those who may not understand those feelings? How do we write of feelings we experience making love? Watching the sun set? Walking along a soft and sandy beach?

We try explaining feelings of fear, anger, happiness, love, excitement, enthusiasm, sadness, depression, etc. But, words cannot express the impact of what we feel.

Words seem most useful to describe situations that create feelings. Pictures, movies and TV commercials help us better experience emotions. But, books, films and advertisements are not feelings. We alone create feelings and emotions, the traits that make us human.

When we discover our unlimited human potential, we best understand this concept of creating our own feelings. Unlimited human potential is, in fact, a feeling, an emotion.

We may have difficulty explaining our experience of unlimited human potential. So, we ought not try. Not struggle searching for the words.

We just need to know that it is a part of us. That we can let it happen.

We don't have to do anything. It is not a do, do, do to get, get, get kind of thing. We don't have to labor to experience unlimited human potential. We just have to start becoming. Allowing it to happen.

The transformation we experience with unlimited human potential is uniquely ours. Even though, for example, I can express the discovery And experience of unlimited human potential for me, I know that your discovery and experience of unlimited human potential will be different. Uniquely your own.

Just like other feelings are. Take a moment and focus on the word "Christmas," for example. What do you feel? Is it happiness? excitement? warmth? a loving memory? Is it sadness? anger? fear? a tragic time? Does the word conjure up no feelings at all because it is not something we celebrate?

Christmas is only one word in a world filled with words. Each one of which elicits a unique experience for each one of us. We are different and, just as we experience the word Christmas differently, we will experience unlimited human potential in our own unique way.

Also, what we experience as unlimited human potential today may be a different experience tomorrow. Discovering and experiencing feelings and emotions, like unlimited human potential, is an unending process which we will never complete.

Let's allow ourselves an opportunity to discover and to experience our own unlimited human potential. Let's let it happen.☐

Hostages and Unlimited Human Potential

I wonder what it's like to be a hostage. To be in a strange country without family and friends, unsure that I would ever see people I loved again. I wonder what it's like to contemplate being tortured, starved, drugged or killed—to live each day focused on what I need to do to stay alive and sane. What must it feel like to concentrate on avoiding hopelessness and helplessness—to ask or to try not asking, "Why is this happening to me?" "Why me?"

Terry Anderson and other men and women who were held hostage for many years all have a unique perspective on the experience. Yet, each one of them found a way to look within for courage, strength, faith, God, trust, understanding, acceptance, compassion and love. Each hostage has his or her own reasons, explanations and descriptions of what happened. But, there is no doubt in my mind, that they each discovered their unlimited human potential. They had to. How else could they have survived and thrived?

Many—not all—walked away from their experiences enriched and empowered. While some did not survive, others were enriched. While some made it through with great difficulty—some of which continued long after their return—others were empowered.

How can it be that some say they are grateful for the experience. They had no jobs or hobbies to go to for distraction. They had no money or possessions. They could not talk over feelings with family or friends. They experienced isolation, true aloneness. They knew physical, emotional and mental abuse.

They went inside themselves and they experienced unlimited human potential. They allowed it to happen. To permeate their entire being. And for this, they were enriched and empowered.➤

We Have to Have It
To Give It Away

*F*or unlimited human potential to become a tangible part of our lives—for us to be able to give it to others and for us to be able to receive it from others—we have to first discover it in ourselves.

To fully experience unlimited human potential and all that it can do for us in our lives, we must begin with loving ourselves. There is no other route.

When we are able to love ourselves, to accept ourselves and to be compassionate with ourselves, we become loving, accepting and compassionate towards others.

We complete the unlimited human potential cycle when we are able to receive it from others.

Firstly, we acknowledge our own unlimited human potential; secondly, we acknowledge it in others; and, lastly, we receive it from others.

This is the way it works.

It is also the way romantic love works, the way relationships thrive. Firstly, we love ourselves; secondly, we love our partners; and, lastly, we receive love from our partners. Relationships fail when one partner does not love self. When one partner expects love from the other one.

I believe that when we discover unlimited human potential in ourselves then we are truly happy. We have inner peace.

Once we acknowledge that unlimited human potential exists in all of us, we can begin developing our own unlimited human potential at are own pace. While unlimited human potential is universal in nature, it is a unique experience for each one of us. As each of us begins to love, accept and be compassionate with ourselves, life seems magical.

The key is to start, to begin right where we are today.

Accept ourselves with love and compassion today and our capacity for love and compassion becomes unlimited. Our ability to acknowledge unlimited human potential in others becomes possible. We can look at other people, especially those who are very different from us and we can allow them to be where they are in terms of their own unlimited human potential awareness. We can be more loving, accepting and compassionate.

But for us to do that—for us to give something away—we must first have it for ourselves. We must love ourselves. ❖

Acceptance

Stop Judging

I moved back to Milwaukee in 1982 when I decided to return to school for a new career. While Orville knew I had accomplished quite a bit during the first six years of our friendship, he was quick to point out to me that I already had three major failures. I didn't make it with the New York Jets; my first marriage ended in divorce; and my two-year stint as a high school head coach had been anything but spectacular with a 3-17 win/loss record.

Orville would kid me about these events and I believed that they did represent failures. I wasn't down on myself exactly, but, I did accept that I had these three major life failures and that no matter what happened in the future, they would always be a part of me.

We all have experiences we don't plan on, experiences we don't like. But, none of them needs to be judged as some sort of failures on our part. I don't believe, in fact, that there is any such thing as failure.

To judge ourselves as failures is limiting. It solves nothing and may set us up for further undesirable experiences.

Life is a never-ending series of actions and results. For every action, there is a result. For every behavior, an outcome. Results or outcomes are simply experiences. They are not good or bad. Not right or wrong. Results and outcomes don't determine whether we are winners or losers, successes or failures. That is a judgment.

And, yes, I do believe it's just as limiting to judge results or outcomes as being "good" as it is to judge them as being "bad."

If we can observe and experience life without judging, interpreting, analyzing and labeling, our experiences will be limitless.

Have you ever noticed that what we thought was a good event at the time it happened turned out later not to have been? And, also, how many times have we thought an event was "bad" and discovered when time had passed that, because it happened, other events occurred which we view positively.

Judgmental thinking keeps us stuck; our experience of life is limited.

When we are able to let go and accept everything, everybody—ourselves—just the way they and we are, then our experience of life is enhanced. ☯

Maybe

*T*he following has been paraphrased from several different seminar leaders as well as from several books. The
original author appears to be unknown.

> *There once lived a poor man who supported his family
> farming. One day, the man's only horse ran away. When
> his neighbor heard the news, he said, "Oh, how unfor-
> tunate you are." The poor man replied, "Maybe."*
>
> *A day or two later, the lost stallion returned leading a
> large herd of wild horses right into the poor man's corral
> As he closed a rickety wooden gate after them, the poor
> man's neighbor hurried to greet him. "How lucky you
> are," he shouted jubilantly. The poor man replied,
> "Maybe."*
>
> *Weeks later, while the poor man's son was breaking in
> one of the family's new horses, the teenager was thrown,
> fracturing his leg. "Such a tragedy," the neighbor la-
> mented. "Maybe," the poor man answered.*
>
> *When some months had passed, a war broke out in the
> poor man's country. Soldiers canvassed farms to draft
> needed young men into the King's Army to fight the
> enemy. Because of the boy's injured leg, he was exempt
> from the draft and, unlike his friends, was not required
> to join. "How fortunate," exclaimed the neighbor.
> "Maybe," said the poor man.*

The poor man did not judge. He understood that nothing is
good or bad. Nothing is right or wrong. Everything just is.

This is freedom. Limitlessness.

My friend Orville's repeated suggestion that I had three
major life failures was not an accurate assessment of me or my

life's events. What I did experience with the New York Jets, my first marriage and my coaching job were a matter of results and outcomes. They were no different than other experiences I have had. Experiences which have led me to where I am today.

And, where I am today is not good or bad. It isn't right or wrong. I do not consider myself a success or a failure. Where I am is where I am. No more and no less.

Where each of us is today is simply that. We aren't failures. We have had a series of experiences which have brought us to where we are, period.

I believe that if we can accept ourselves today just the way we are, then we can—we will—look back at all of our life experiences with appreciation. It is those experiences that have allowed us to become who we are this very minute.

If we judge ourselves and, in that judging, find fault with who we are today, we will look back and find someone or something to blame for those faults. We may choose not to blame anyone but ourselves. But, whether we choose to blame others or ourselves isn't important. The fact is that if we blame anyone at all, we are not accepting ourselves.

It's vital that we accept ourselves just the way we are today. In fact, if we today find ourselves finding fault with who we are, we should just accept that.

Without judgment.

When we begin the process of accepting ourselves completely and totally—when we eliminate judging ourselves or our pasts—we become happy, peaceful and unlimited. As unlimited as we are today.□

We Can't Understand

I've caught myself saying, "I understand how you feel" more times than I can remember. While I've said those words, they are not true. I can never understand how anyone feels. Just like no one can ever understand how I feel. We can "try" to understand each other. We can try to put ourselves in another person's position. But all we do is try. When it comes to truly understanding how someone else feels, we can't do it.

I will never see the world through your eyes and you will never see the world through mine. I think, then, that we ought to stop trying to understand. That we ought to just begin accepting.

When we try to understand how someone feels, we imagine ourselves in their position. The feelings we then generate are the feelings we would have if we were in their situation. The feelings we have, in other words, are not the feelings that the other person has. They are only OUR understanding of how WE might feel if we were experiencing what they are experiencing. *When we're trying to understand how others feel, we put ourselves in the position of judging others because we base what they're feeling or should be feeling on what we might feel.*

When we begin accepting the feelings of others without trying to understand them, we stop judging them.

Parents try to understand their children and children try to understand their parents. Employers try to understand their employees and employees try to understand their employers. Men try to understand women and women try to understand men. Whites try to understand blacks and blacks try to understand whites. Different races and countries try understanding each other.

It doesn't work.

Trying to understand leads to frustration, confusion, miscommunication and resentment.

What's more, trying to understand sometimes becomes destructive, particularly when we ASSUME we understand. When an individual, race, group or country assumes it understands another individual, race, group or country, it begins deciding what the other side SHOULD feel or how they SHOULD act or behave. This posture results in fear, prejudice, hate and, oftentimes, war.

I can never understand what it is like to be a black or a woman or a gay person. I can never understand what it's like to be homeless or starving in India. I cannot understand, but I can accept. I can't understand, but I can radiate compassion and love. I will not understand, but I can empathize.➤

Empathy

*E*mpathy is acceptance with love and compassion. We may not be able to understand the feelings others are having, but we can empathize with them.

Empathizing is not pitying. It does not ignore the situation any one is in. It allows us to handle any situation. Empathy gives us freedom. It gives others freedom.

While it would be nice to live in a world without fear, hate and prejudice, this is not the case. While it would be nice to every day be surrounded by people who are loving, accepting and compassionate, this is also not the case.

I feel tremendous empathy for the struggle waged by women, blacks, gays and other groups who only ask to be allowed to live without judgment and persecution. Wanting just to be treated equally.

While it's not easy for me, I also need to have empathy for those who do hate, judge and condemn others.

Empathy is not a one-way street. It's not a matter of having empathy for those we like and not for those we dislike. To practice acceptance is to accept everyone and everything. Individuals and groups who seem the most difficult for us to accept are those who need our acceptance the most.

Individuals and groups who are the most difficult to love are those who need our love the most. This is exactly as it should be.

It may seem ironic, but, we must realize that to live in a world where there is only love, acceptance and compassion, we must love, accept and be compassionate towards individuals and groups who do not display these characteristics.

To live in a world free of fear, prejudice and hate, we must begin loving, accepting and being compassionate towards individuals and groups who are fearful, who are prejudiced, who hate. ❖

It's Not the Same

A friend of mine grew up in a large city. He is white, but was part of a minority when he attended high school in the 1970's. The majority of his classmates were black.

My friend graduated from high school and college and is currently involved in a successful business venture.

One day, when he was talking about his high school days, my friend became upset and irritated, almost mad. He told me that only a handful of his several hundred black high school classmates had actually "made it." My friend was frustrated. He had made it, he said, but the majority of his black counterparts had not.

He had grown up in the same environment as they did, he explained. He had become successful. Why hadn't they?

My friend is a nice guy. He has TRIED TO UNDERSTAND. He has tried putting himself in their situation. In his mind, he knows exactly what it is to be in their situation because he grew up in the same poor neighborhoods and attended the very same schools.

But, my friend will never understand what it's like to be black.

And, as long as he continues to try to understand, he will continue to become confused, frustrated and prejudiced when he talks about his struggling black classmates.

We should stop trying to understand why people make particular choices. When we—my friend, you or me—try to understand why people make choices that we wouldn't necessarily make in the same or similar situations, we become confused and judgmental.

Life is easier—less frustrating—when we accept others just the way they are. Accepting others with love and compassion frees us from confusion, frustration and judgment.☯

Complete Acceptance

I have friend who hates homosexuals. He won't discuss the issue and says he is entitled to his opinion which, he says, is "I hate gays period."

I'm not gay and I can never understand anyone who is. I don't try understanding gays. I do accept them. I am not a person who hates gays and I can't understand someone who does. But, I do accept them, too.

The concept of accepting, like empathizing, is not something we can do in one direction but not in another. We can't exclusively accept people and causes we happen to believe in and let it go at that. A difficult but vital way to live is to be more accepting in all circumstances.

If we are pro-black, pro-gay or pro-whatever, are we able to accept anti-black (like the Ku Klux Klansmen), anti-gay (like the Skinheads) and anti-whatever else? It is difficult for me, especially when I consider examples like the ones I used for these examples represent groups known to be violent. Groups who do not accept others, remember, are those who need acceptance the most.

Not everyone who is anti-black or anti-gay is prone to violence. In fact, the majority of people who are anti-black or anti-gay are non-violent. They just cannot accept.

It's impossible to look at someone and determine his or her belief system. It's even more impossible to try to understand them. When we stop labeling, analyzing, interpreting and judging, we will accept everyone.

Until this happens, the world will continue to be a confusing, frustrating and difficult place.

We can accept the world just the way it is. Everything that is happening in every corner of the universe is supposed to be happening.

This concept of accepting versus understanding is also supposed to be happening.

The only way we can change anything is to accept everything. Then and only then will change be possible.◻

A Tablemate

I went on a cruise recently. One of the main enjoyments was food. I ate my meals at large tables, where I was seated with people I didn't know before boarding.

One of my tablemates was a woman I didn't care for but was able to accept. I spent no time trying to understand her. No time analyzing or interpreting or labeling her. I did not concern myself with changing her or with pointing out to her those traits I didn't like.

I did not consume myself with trying to figure out why she said the things she said or did the things she did that seemed to cause others at the table some dismay.

I accepted her. I communicated my acceptance, but did not spend time with her.

Accepting someone or something does not mean you are required to like that person or thing. I didn't care for one of the women at my table so I chose to spend as little time with her as I could, while still communicating acceptance when I was with her. She is a human being and she deserves acceptance for just being alive.➤

Accepting Versus Liking

*M*y mother devotes herself to volunteer work throughout the City of Milwaukee. One morning, during one of my frequent visits, I talked with her about the concept of acceptance.

I told her I accepted poverty, homelessness and starvation. Her reaction was disbelief. How could I, she wanted to know, accept such horrible conditions?

Acceptance doesn't mean I like any of those conditions. Accepting isn't necessarily passive.

Accepting a situation makes it easier to do something about it. Accepting poverty, homelessness and starvation doesn't mean we will ignore them. If we are motivated to do something about any of those conditions—as my mother is—we will do something.

If we cannot accept someone or some situation, there is little we can or will do about them.

Before change can happen, we must accept. It's ironic. When we accept someone or something moment-to-moment, we are not obsessed with change, with trying, with struggling.

Yet, this is precisely when change takes place. ❖

Expecting

*J*ust as we need to be accepting instead of understanding, we also need to be accepting instead of expecting.

When we expect people to be or events to turn out in a prescribed way, we are often disappointed. This is because our expectations are usually based on our own beliefs, our own , our own understanding and our own viewpoint.

When someone or something doesn't meet our expectations, we are disappointed, frustrated and confused. These are the same results we get when we try to understand.

Motivational speakers and seminar instructors tell us that it's important to expect some desired result if we are to succeed, if we are to be fulfilled. This is fine. I do believe that desiring a specific outcome or imagining some specific result is empowering—but it's empowering only when we can also accept whatever outcome or result does happen.

The word "expect" feels demanding to me. It's sounds like a command. But, we live in the 1990's and commands don't work for most of us.

Expecting our wives to iron our shirts or prepare nightly dinners may present a huge problem if those jobs don't fit into her plans. Expecting husbands to be sole breadwinners or the ones to shoulder the major financial responsibilities in a family may present a problem if those jobs don't fit into his plans.

If a woman or a man wants to do shirts and prepare every dinner, that's fine. If a man or woman wants to shoulder the family's financial responsibilities, that's fine, too. But, these jobs ought to be performed because the individual performing them wants to do them—not because their mate expects them to perform them.

When acceptance is a part of who we are and how we live, life is freeing. We eliminate unnecessary problems and unpleasant confrontations.

Acceptance works because we are never disappointed. Put another way, we are never disappointed because acceptance works.

Becoming 100 percent accepting is difficult. *When we find ourselves disappointed, confused or frustrated, we can be sure that we have either been expecting or been trying to understand some person or situation.*

When we feel disappointment, confusion or frustration and we recognize that we are not being accepting, we mustn't become upset with ourselves. This is a perfect time to accept who we are. To accept ourselves and our situation.

We may desire to be more accepting in our lives and that is fine. But, accepting ourselves moment to moment is our key to freedom.

As we become more self-accepting, we will become more accepting of others. Eventually, what we do becomes automatic.

Expect Nothing. Accept Everything.

All of us grow and change differently.

We should love ourselves and others enough to allow change to happen. We should decrease our desire to expect change and begin just allowing it to happen.

Expect nothing. Accept everything.☯

Accepting Ourselves First

*O*ne of the primary reasons many of us don't easily accept others is related to the difficulty we have accepting ourselves. We may not like who or what we are at this moment in time. I'm not talking about those of us who hate ourselves; those of us who see every minute of every day as an enormous struggle. I'm talking about those of us who simply don't accept where we are right now. Who are unhappy with ourselves.

We've been taught—programmed to believe—that we will not be fulfilled until we accomplish certain tasks. We believe that we cannot accept ourselves until we increase our education base, earn at a greater income level, reach a particular status in our jobs or careers, find an appropriate mate and get married, have 2.5 children, etc. What we've been taught interferes with our self-acceptance and it's easy to see that if we continue "buying into" these subtle lessons, we will always have more things on our to do lists than can be accomplished before self-acceptance takes place. Always.

There's nothing wrong with accomplishment. It's fine to set goals and achieve them.

But, for us to tap into our unlimited human potential, we must accept ourselves totally and completely today—no matter where we are on life's journey.

As we become increasingly self-accepting, we naturally begin accepting others. It's a rather simplistic principle: We must accept ourselves before we can accept others; we just cannot accept others until we accept us.

If we decide to accept some people in some situations, but not all people in all situations, we limit ourselves. When we place stipulations and expectations on others, we can be sure we are placing them on ourselves.

We limit ourselves and our life's experiences by not accepting ourselves right here and right now. Whatever we are doing to our ourselves, we are doing to others.

To experience our unlimited human potential, we must be completely accepting of who we are today. Not tomorrow—after we achieve this or that —but today just as we are this moment. When we do this for ourselves, we can and will experience the unlimited human potential in us and in others.

None of this takes place overnight. We must have patience.

Changes that may or may not take place in us are determined by us individually. There is no right or wrong way. There is just who we are.

As always, wherever and whatever and whoever we happen to be at this moment is already perfect. It's not necessary to make some change to be perfect. We already are perfect—as human beings. All of our decisions, choices and behaviors may not be perfect. Let us accept our imperfections but not judge ourselves less than perfect as human beings.

I believe that if we are not happy—if we are struggling—we must just accept that about ourselves first. Change will happen.

As we accept ourselves more and more as each day passes, we accept others naturally. Change is automatic. It doesn't need to be forced; it won't be forced. We will, I know, just become more happy, more fulfilled. We will not struggle.

Unlimited human potential is natural. It is within us all. Accept yourself and just let it happen.◻

Two Paths to Acceptance

S ome of us have self-limiting beliefs. I am fat, we say. Or, I am ugly. Or, I am a loser. Or, I am a failure. For those of us who make these kinds of statements, acceptance is not a problem at all. Our acceptance—our self-limiting acceptance— is already developed and in place. But, it is not the empowering kind of acceptance that frees us.

"It's just the way I am" or "It's just the way things are" represent acceptance we don't need. This kind of acceptance is an excuse to avoid change. Self-limiting beliefs just immobilize us. They allow us to stay stuck. If we buy into self-limiting acceptance, we don't—we won't—take any action at all. Why would we if we believe "That's just the way it is."

Limiting self-beliefs occur when we don't experience self-love or self-compassion. *A lack of self-love and self-compassion is the root cause of our lack of self esteem.* And, where does this emanate from? I don't know because there are a multitude of explanations out there. The list is infinite. Anyone can justify their circumstances. Anyone can blame and point outwardly for their lack of self-love, self-compassion, self-esteem. It doesn't matter, really, what the rationale is. We are where we are because that is where we are.

The choice to be accepting can, then, lead us down two very different paths.

One path accepts where we are based upon what other people have done to us, the environment we were brought up in—things we did not choose. This kind of acceptance is immobilizing. It forces us to give up, to quit, to be stuck.

The second path accepts where we are and looks neither outward nor inward for excuses or blame. This is the path that just accepts. This path is mobilizing. It's freeing and limitless. It's empowering.

If we choose the first path—the one that looks to external forces for self-limiting acceptance—we will be inclined to look outwardly for change to happen. We will look to have change done TO us. Our ability to change or to take action will be determined by other people, other events.

When we choose the second path, we unconditionally accept ourselves for being who we are. We know we alone determine whether we will or won't change or whether action will or will not take place.➤

Reality Check

Relationships and the World

*R*elationships involve two people, an entire family, our work environment, cities, countries and the world. From our observations of relationships, we can see in the dynamics of relationships two extremes in human behavior. We can see love and we can see fear, which is the absence of love.

When little Bobby doesn't want to share his new red truck with his baby sister, she becomes upset. Bobby is selfish—afraid or, rather, in fear of losing something. Jenny, his sister, is jealous—envious, or rather, in fear of not getting something. She may use guilt to get what she wants in the form of "pity, poor me." In this sibling interaction, we see a clear lack of love, acceptance and compassion. Maybe Jenny will tug at the truck and break it. Bobby will cry and blame Jenny for breaking his toy. He may hit her. She will cry and run to Mommy. Mommy will confront them and they will both relay their interpretations and justifications of what took place. They will believe each is right. Both will rationalize their thoughts and their actions.

Let's look at divorce, a common event in our country. Mom and Dad disagree. They rationalize why each is right and the other is wrong. They take some of the same actions Bobby and Jenny do with the truck. A judge is called in.

In the business world, partners have a difficult time working together. One feels he is doing more than the other one. Or, one doesn't like the actions or inactions taken by the other one. Both want something. Lawyers are called in.

Justifications are recorded. Juries are asked to decide.

A worker feels he is doing better or more work than another, but not getting paid as much to perform. One is using sick leave

119

when he's not sick. He's discussing his personal problems with the boss and this angers the other one. One feels deprived of something the other one has. Each believes he is right and the other is wrong. The boss is called in to decide what's fair and what isn't.

Looking at a broader picture, we can use Iraq and Kuwait as an example. Two countries with differences, each wanting something. The United States entered their conflict to protect its interests (oil) and to do for them what Mommy was asked to do with Bobby and Jenny, what a judge was asked to do for Mom and Dad, a jury was asked to do for business partners, what the boss had to do with her employees.

Let's look at our communities. When there is talk of widening a road, we find those for it and those against it, each with their own reasons and rationale. Both groups believing they are right. Each wanting something. Each fearing the loss of something.

Relationship dynamics can be translated or extrapolated from a city's example to a state's, from state to country, country to the world.

Observe behavior and trace it back. You'll find love or the absence of love. Even with what appears to be a worldwide, enormous and complicated situation, we can see in it Bobby and Jenny and Mommy.

We can see in it Mom, Dad and a judge. We can see partners and juries. Co-workers and bosses.

We can see in all our arguments fear, judgment, jealousy, guilt, hate, blame, etc. We see someone believing he or she is right and the other is wrong. We see negative thoughts, feelings and behaviors.

We see the absence of love, compassion and acceptance. ❖

Perfectly Okay

*D*riving home from my office one evening, I was tuned into a radio talk show discussion on teenage violence. Callers and host, an opinionated personality with a reputation for stirring-up his audiences, were angry. Their dialogue, which focused on why this kind of behavior occurred and what callers thought should be done to stop it, was heated. The more they talked about it, the greater their agitation seemed to grow.

I imagined myself dialing up the host and telling him and his radio audience all I thought about unlimited human potential. All about our inner core. A core brimming with love, acceptance and compassion. I heard me telling everyone who was tuned in, that, while some teenagers may behave inappropriately, we must look inside them for their goodness. Look beyond their violent acts.

Time out. Hold everything. Let me speak the truth.

I really did not feel that way. While I listened to the radio and the dialogue from victims of teenage violence, I felt angry and confused. I felt some of the same feelings the other callers expressed.

Had I called in talking of love, acceptance and compassion, though, I am sure I wouldn't have received a welcoming response. I don't think they would have heard me and I wouldn't have "blamed" them for that. There is a time and a place for everything.

What I wish I had said—things about unlimited human potential—would have been inappropriate. As inappropriate as if I had suggested to the loved ones of a murder victim that they should, a moment after a such a tragedy, forgive and forget.

Who, I wonder, doesn't get angry? Who doesn't get confused or frustrated some of the time? There may be some individuals able to control themselves 100% of the time, but I don't know too many of them. The vast majority of us are likely to feel and express our anger.

This is true even though we know, intellectually, that there isn't much point to having and expressing these emotions. Even though we know that becoming upset and angry never changes what's already happened.

Reacting to tragedy with love, acceptance and compassion is wonderful. But, it is perfectly okay to get mad. It's okay to speak out, to say what's on our minds.☯

We're All Okay Just the Way We Are

J am not a Tibetan monk. I am not a pacifist.

I am aggressive and competitive. I have a rather intimidating personality. I live in the real world. I witness injustice, pain, hardship.

I am aware that the world and the people in it are not always loving, accepting and compassionate. Some are never loving, accepting and compassionate.

I can sometimes easily become upset, angry or disappointed. I would require a tremendous infusion of love, acceptance and compassion to even begin comprehending an Adolf Hitler, a Sadam Hussein, a Jeffrey Dahmer. For me to comprehend the racism, hate, irreverence for human life that today exists in our world.

> ### *You Can Only Change You*

I bring this up to let you know I do not live on a mountaintop where I observe and judge the world.

I am a lot like you.

I live in the same world you live in. I may continue being aggressive, competitive and intimidating forever. I may continue becoming easily upset, angry or disappointed even as I grow in awareness. You may continue feeling or expressing those emotions too.

It's okay. Be who you are because who you are is fine. Do what you do because doing what you do is fine. We all need to do what we need to do. To be what we need to be.

I don't want to change you or the world. I can only change me. You can only change you.

This is what I want you to know.◻

Love and the Workplace

*W*hen I decided to write down my thoughts and produce seminars on love, acceptance and compassion, I was told that the topic wouldn't fly in the corporate world. Not because it was wrong and not because it wouldn't help. Because the corporate world, an audience I wanted to address with these materials, wasn't ready to hear about love, acceptance and compassion in the workplace.

Corporate leaders, I was told, believe that hard work and discipline are the real—if not the only—paths to productivity, profit and success. No one believes he or she made it to CEO because of love, acceptance or compassion. No business executive would be comfortable talking about these things. And, lastly, none would be willing to hug or to love their co-workers and employees.

I accepted my advisors' concerns before I thoroughly explored all I had to say about love, acceptance and compassion in the workplace and in society as a whole. Those words, I know, are powerful. They are normally associated with strong emotions. But, there is no universal definition of love, acceptance and compassion. There are numerous individual representations of what the words mean to us depending on what has happened to us in our lives.

I believe, then, that it's is my responsibility to communicate what love means to me and how it can be valued in the workplace.

For most of us, it's difficult to transpose the love we have for our partners and family to the workplace or to society as a whole. How can that kind of love fit in with co-workers, bosses, employees or other associates, people we don't know personally or intimately.

Love is an attitude. An approach. An emotion. It's not something we do to someone.

Love is helping others to be who and what they want to be, not what we want them to be—what THEY want to be. Decisions affecting people we work with can be made in an atmosphere of love, in an atmosphere replete with helping them be all they can be.

Does love mean we can't get angry with employees? Can't fire them if we need to. No, it doesn't.

Parents love their children and still get angry with them. The anger may result in discipline of and, sometimes, penalties for their children. When we approach with love, the action we take is for the ultimate benefit of our children. This is the way it ought to be with our employees.

What do we do when our employees are not performing well? When we've provided all the help we can to them without positive response on their part and when they are negatively affecting other workers, what can we do? We can fire them. But, if we approach them with love, we won't fire them after we've become disgusted and angry. We won't fire them on the spot for some transgression or another even if that will benefit our company or our other employees.

A loving approach would be to sit down with them and explain that we've tried to help but we can see that it's not working for either of us. A scenario like this can benefit everyone. The fired employee may or may not respond positively to this approach. That is out of our control. But, we can let love be our approach and our chances that things will work out will greatly improve.

When we discipline our children through love, they may or may not be happy with us at the time, But, when our discipline is based on helping them—not on helping ourselves—the decision to discipline will work out. Eventually, they will know this, too.

Our decisions as employees, bosses, co-workers or family members must be based on benefiting the other person. Our decisions are made for them. Not for what we think is best for them. For what will benefit them.

Keeping this in mind helps us make loving decisions. When we're unsure, we can ask ourselves, "Who will this decision benefit?"➤

Love Everyone?
Impossible. Maybe Not.

*W*e love sunsets, the smell of flowers, the brightness of stars, chocolate ice cream, sensitive movies and pepperoni pizza. I use the word in this book as freely as most people do. I use it to define unlimited human potential.

What feelings do we get when we define what love means to us? Who do we think about when we explain love? Is it our partners, our mothers, our fathers, our children, good friends, our pets?

Are we filled with compassion and inner peace when we think about the people we love and the people who love us? Probably, the answer is yes.

The thoughts, feelings and emotions we have when we think of those we love make it difficult to understand the meaning of the word when someone says we ought to love our neighbors or love our enemies.

How can we love people we don't like? How can we love an enemy—someone we know doesn't love us? How can we love people who hurt us or hurt others? How can we love Democrats when we are Republicans, Republicans when we are Democrats? How we can love male chauvinists when we are feminists, liberals when we are conservatives and vice versa? How, indeed, can we love thieves, muggers, murderers, rapists or child molesters?

Our core, our true nature, our unlimited human potential is love, compassion and acceptance.

We can probably accept and offer compassion to these others, but we will likely object to loving them.

127

Why? Because of the feelings we have when we define the word. Because of what we think the word means.

How could we possibly feel the same kinds of feelings toward murderers that we feel toward our children? We can't.

I struggled with this concept until I recognized that love is not something we do to or for someone—it's not hugging them, kissing them, praising them and so forth. It's not always an overwhelming feeling of joy and peace.

る

Love is the absence of *hate*

Love is the absence of *fear*

Love is the absence of *blame*

Love is the absence of *judgment*

Love is the absence of *prejudice*

Love is the absence of *guilt.*

る

With this revised definition of the word love, I can acknowledge love for all people. We don't have to love all people the same way we love those who are close to us. We can love all people simply because they are people. People doing the best they can based on their present levels of awareness. Human beings on the wheel of life, making choices and living with the consequences of those choices whatever they may be. Human beings facing obstacles and challenges every day of their lives.❖

Processing Life's Events

What's Normal

"Dysfunctional" has become a popular term in the last few years. It's used to describe a family unit which isn't "normal."

What is normal? Is there such a thing as a normal, functional family? If so, are there abnormal, dysfunctional families?

While the word "dysfunctional" may be a nicer label than "bad," "lousy" and . . . "screwed up," it's used in the same way that those words might be.

I don't believe there is any such entity as a dysfunctional family. I also don't believe there is any such entity as a functional family.

I believe there just is.

Many of us have grown up in homes with alcoholism, incest, mental and emotional abuse. Many of us have experienced devastating childhoods. But, I think, in-depth interviews with every being on earth would reveal that, in one way or another, each of us—100% of us—have experienced situations that could be labeled "dysfunctional" or "abnormal."

I trust that we could each look at who we are today and point a finger toward our "dysfunctional" families for our perceived flaws.

I am not making light of our difficult childhood experiences. I accept that we may be experiencing difficulties in our present because of our past. I am not judging us.

I am suggesting, though, that we let go of the idea that a dysfunctional past results in—equates to—a dysfunctional present.

Why? Because if we don't let go, our dysfunctional pasts and our dysfunctional presents—if that's the label we're using — will lead us straight into dysfunctional futures.

I know we can't change our pasts, but I do know we can change how we view them. We don't, in fact, want to change our pasts. For our past is part of who we are today. And, who we are today is perfect.

What I'm suggesting is changing how we process our past. Our past isn't "good or bad," not "right or wrong." It just is.☯

A Different View

*W*e can process our past in such a way that it becomes a stepping stone to a happy, peaceful and unlimited now.

Like the stories of two young men introduced below, each of us has our own way of processing our pasts. None is right or wrong. None is good or bad.

As we read these stories, we can see that one way of processing our past leads to freedom and limitlessness. Another leads to struggle and unhappiness.

STORY #1

I was the last of four children. I was not planned. I was an afterthought. My brother and sisters were in college when I was growing up and I was very lonely. My father was older and didn't spend much time with me. My mother, who had spent most of her life raising my brother and sisters, decided to return to work while I was growing up.

I did poorly in school and didn't have many friends. I was terribly overweight, had a poor self-image and did little dating in high school. College wasn't much different. I majored in education even though I didn't want to be a teacher. Girls didn't fall all over me so my social life was limited. After finally graduating in five years, I met someone who must have been pretty hard-up because she married me. The marriage lasted for one year before she left me. My sisters are both divorced and my parents didn't have a great marriage either. It probably runs in the family.

133

I was a high school football coach who compiled a 3-17 win-loss record and was fired from coaching after my second year.

I quit teaching and went back to school. I got married again and I got divorced again. I started my own business which is holding its own, but with a past like mine, I doubt that I will ever be successful or happy.

STORY #2

I was the baby. Everyone in my family doted over me. They spoiled me. My brother, who is seven years older than I am spent a lot of time with me. He was my idol. I remember watching the Green Bay Packers on TV and, at every half-time, going outside and throwing a football around with him. I remember playing slow motion football in our side yard and rustling in the fallen autumn leaves. I remember being very happy when I was a child.

My mother and father were supportive. They weren't critical of my school work at all and always encouraged me. They didn't compare me to my brother or sisters and just let me be me. I didn't date much in high school. I just wasn't ready. I did have a special friendship with a guy in my history class. We did practically everything together. I'm sure I spent more time at his house than I did at my own. His mom and dad were my second set of parents.

I was fortunate to excel in football and to receive a full four-year athletic college scholarship. I achieved my master's degree while I worked as a part-time college football coach. And, I met a nice, attractive and intelligent young woman whom I married. We were on different paths and, when we recognized that, our relationship ended.

I was the youngest head coach for high school football in my county. My record, over the two years I served as coach, wasn't what I would like to have achieved, but the experience taught me a lot about myself and about human behavior. I learned that being a coach was not something I wished to pursue.

I went back to school and graduated with honors. I met a wonderful woman and got married again. She was different than anyone else I'd ever dated and taught me to open up and view the world from other perspectives.

134

We found ourselves on different paths and ended the marriage, but, to that partnership, I attribute much of what helped shape who I am today.

My oldest sister taught me that it is never too late for happiness. My older sister taught me about what it's like to be a woman in a male-dominated world. She helped me accept all people—no matter what their color.

I started and operate a business that is fun and rewarding. It gives me free time to study the world I live in and to learn about myself. Like everyone else, I have "problems." But, I consider them to be challenges, just a part of what life is all about.

I met a perfect woman a few years ago and am married again. She is everything I need and want. We are on different paths, but they seem to run together. I am happy today. And I believe that today is all there is.

If you haven't already guessed, story 1 and story 2 are reflections of the same person's life from different views. I am who the stories are about and the second version expresses my "real" viewpoint of my life—the way I have chosen to process my history—at this moment in time.

I'm not suggesting that it's easy to change the way we process our experiences. I'm not at all suggesting that we make light of our particular situations. I am hoping to just relay that other possibilities exist. Possibilities that can free us.

Just because events have occurred in the past doesn't preclude us from changing the way we process those events today. We do have choices. We can begin looking at things differently any time we choose to.❒

Reality—Objective and Subjective

*I*n the book *Ordinary Moments*, Dan Millman introduced the concepts of objective and subjective . Objective , he said, is what is physically happening. Subjective is our interpretations, beliefs and perceptions of what is physically happening.

Objective can be considered true . Subjective is the one true in our own minds.

No two people have the same interpretations, beliefs and perceptions. No two people, therefore, share the same .

"BOB & CAROL"

Physical :

> Bob and Carol were married for one year. Bob came home from work at 7 P.M. Carol was not at home, but her car was in the garage. Bob placed a TV dinner in the microwave, walked over to the front window and peered out. He read the newspaper. He walked over to the window and looked out again. He ate his dinner, watched television and went to bed.

Subjective :

> Bob's thoughts, scenario 1: It's 7 P.M., where is she? She should be home fixing my dinner. I wonder where she is? Maybe she's having an affair. She's with the church choir director, I just know it. Why is she doing this to me? What did I do to deserve this? I'll have to eat a lousy TV dinner. That little tramp. I might as well read the depressing

newspaper. Where is she? I still don't see her coming. Heck, I'll watch some stupid TV and go to bed. I don't care if she ever comes home.

Bob's thoughts, scenario 2: I wonder why Carol isn't home? Oh, my God, I'll bet something bad has happened to her. She's been in an accident. A horrible accident. No. Maybe someone raped her and then kidnaped her. I'll eat something so I won't think about it. I'll read the paper and watch TV to get my mind off of what's happened. Where could she be? My poor wife. Maybe I should just go to bed and hope she isn't dead or hurt.

Bob's thoughts, scenario 3: Carol isn't home, that's unusual. No note either. Oh well, I might as well fix a TV dinner. I don't see her coming. I certainly hope everything is okay. Well, there isn't anything I can do about it anyway. I might as well read the paper. It's getting late and I wonder why she hasn't called. She must not be near a telephone. I'll watch a little TV and go to bed. I'm sure she's fine. There are probably good reasons why she's not here and why she hasn't called. There's nothing I can do anyway.

These are three scenarios from an unlimited number of possibilities. They aren't good or bad, right or wrong. They're just examples of subjective realities. If we tried to determine the best or worse among them, we would involve ourselves in another subjective . One based on our own individual interpretations, beliefs and perceptions.

It's not important to determine which scenario is "right" anyway; it is important to understand that each one of us creates our own subjective based on our own interpretations, beliefs and perceptions.

Where was Carol? It's not important to determine the true ; it is important to understand that each subjective Bob created was no less real to him—in his mind—than was the objective .

Our thoughts—our interpretations, beliefs and perceptions—create feelings which create emotions which create action or inaction. No matter what we're doing or not doing, no matter what feelings and emotions we're having, we are the ones creating our realities through the thoughts we have at any given time.

Carol didn't "make" Bob think a certain way. She didn't put thoughts into his mind. Carol couldn't do that if she tried. Only Bob can have the thoughts that are in Bob's mind.

This is true for each of us.

If we were to step into any scenario and ask Bob why he was having his particular thoughts, Bob would list several reasons, excuses and justifications. He might even tell us that his parents gave him some of the thoughts he had. Bob's justifications are valid—in his mind—because that's where they all came from. And, we are able to identify with Bob to the point where we share realities with him.

Bob's thoughts, feelings and emotions, though, are Bob's and no one else's. His reasons and justifications are just additional thoughts in his control.

When Bob recognizes that he creates—through the thoughts he has—his own that is separate from what is actually happening for Carol, he begins accepting responsibility for his —for his life.

Bob may continue having the same thoughts, feelings and emotions—he may have the same reasons and justifications for them —but he will know they are his and his alone. If he doesn't like what he's feeling or the action he takes as a result of those feelings, he can, now that he understands and accepts responsibility, change his thoughts.

In scenario 3, Bob was cool, calm and collected. He wasn't angry, upset or worried like he had been in scenarios 1 and 2. Does this mean that scenario 3 is a "more correct" ? That it is a good way to be?

Not necessarily. Scenario #3 just happens to be one way of interpreting, believing and perceiving. It isn't right or wrong, good or bad. It's simply Bob's scenario 3.

While he may not have gotten angry or worried in scenario 3, he didn't take any action. He knew that Carol wasn't at home at a time when she usually would be. Let's suppose she had slipped on some oil in the garage while she was closing her car door. Suppose she had cut her head badly and was unconscious. Bob 3 might not have found her until the next day when it might have been too late to help her.

Bob 2, although worried and erratic, may have run out to the garage during his panic and he may have spotted her on the garage floor. Perhaps he would have saved her life.

We could come up with an unlimited number of possible scenarios and an unlimited number of possible reactions. We could also discuss reasons and justifications for them all day long.

Our thoughts on this day are the sum total of our own genetic makeup and everything that has ever happened to us—both consciously and unconsciously. When we accept responsibility for those thoughts, we accept responsibility for our lives.

This realization is the single most powerful and freeing realization we will ever have. We know that through our thoughts, we have control over our lives. Our responses to whatever challenges, obstacles, situations or people we may come across.

Take a look once again at the objective for Bob and Carol. It's boring, isn't it? Objective without subjective is simply not life.

Our thoughts create richness in our lives.

While we can do nothing about objective, we can do everything about subjective. We can incorporate our own beliefs, interpretations and perceptions into our experience of life.

If we don't like how we are feeling, all we need to do is change our thoughts.➤

Negative Thoughts

*W*e spend time looking at the past to understand our thoughts today. We do this because we know that thoughts create feelings and we are concerned with our feelings. The feelings and emotions that normally cause us to look back into our past are labeled negative.

[I don't know if they should be labeled at all; I'm not fond of identifying things as good or bad, right or wrong, negative or positive, because in the big picture of life, I believe all emotions have a purpose].

In any event, negative emotions are created by those thoughts—those interpretations, beliefs and perceptions—that are not loving, accepting and compassionate.

While all of us have negative thoughts each day, this doesn't mean that we are not loving, accepting and compassionate beings. It's just that when we're having negative thoughts— when we don't like the feelings we're feeling —we can't, during those moments, be loving, accepting and compassionate.

The more negative thoughts we have or the longer we stay stuck thinking, feeling and acting negatively, the less time we spend being loving, accepting and compassionate.

The more time we spend not being loving, accepting and compassionate, the more difficult it becomes to change our negative thinking. We become depressed, fearful, guilty or angry. We are stuck and unhappy.

Getting unstuck isn't easy. We have to work long and hard to change negative thinking. We may reach out to a counselor or clergy person for help. We may read books or talk to friends. But, we will stay stuck until we can change our negative thoughts. And, in the final analysis, no one can change them for us. Only we can do that.

If we must examine our pasts (that is, our perceptions, beliefs and interpretations of what happened), we ought to do it as quickly as we can. For the longer we spend today trying to figure out yesterday, the fewer todays we have to be alive.

We must remember, as I've said elsewhere, that we are who we are today because of all our yesterdays. We can't change our objective pasts. What has happened has happened already. We can, however, change our perceptions, beliefs and interpretations of our pasts by changing the negative thoughts we have today into love, acceptance and compassion.

If we like who we are today—if we are happy and content right now—then we can look at the past with total love, acceptance and compassion because we accept and embrace who we are today in the context of our pasts. We know we are who we are today because of everybody and everything in our past. People and events that we may describe as "bad" are just as much a part of us as people and events that we may describe as "good."

If we don't like who we are today—if we are unhappy and dissatisfied right now—we look to our pasts for the reasons—the negative events—for that unhappiness. We examine people from our pasts to see if they were the ones who caused us to feel unhappy in the present—who it was that "did it" to us. When we're looking at our pasts in this way, we might want to ask ourselves if we are also looking for the good in our pasts. Was everything that happened to us "bad?" We are who we are today, remember, because of everything in our pasts. Both the good and the bad.

The list of events and people in our pasts is endless. Books popular today, many of them quite valuable, seem devoted to having us dwell in our pasts. To helping us understand our pasts. But, we will never completely understand our pasts no matter whose formula we follow. We can, however, accept our pasts. When we are loving, accepting and compassionate with ourselves and others, we don't dwell on the negative aspects of our pasts. When we are loving, accepting and compassionate with ourselves and others, we are more loving, accepting and compassionate about our pasts, too.

Being loving, accepting and compassionate with ourselves and others becomes most possible when we recognize and internalize that everyone is doing the best that he or she can at any given moment in time based on his or her own genetics, past conditioning and current surroundings.

Author Dr. Robert Anthony put it this way, "Every decision you make and every action you take is based on your present level of awareness."

We think what we think, feel what we feel, do what we do based on our present levels of awareness. Our own unique combinations of genetics, past conditioning and current surroundings. Trying to figure out why and what we think, feel and do is futile. Trying to figure out all the elements that come into play in determining why we think and feel the way we do is impossible. It would be easier to pick the winning six numbers for the weekly Florida State Lottery, a game with odds of one-in-14 million.

Our present level of awareness is simply a combination of genetics, past conditioning—both conscious and unconscious—and our current surroundings. Period. This present level of awareness forms the basis for all our thoughts, emotions and behaviors. Everything we are right now—this very second—is based on our present level of awareness.

All our doubts, fears, joys, values, disappointments, grudges, judgments, blames, worries, guilts, victories, defeats, successes, failures, ups, downs, actions and inactions—all—are based on our awareness at this moment in time.

No one, to paraphrase Eleanor Roosevelt, can make us feel unworthy without our consent. ❖

Not Being Alive

I'm a physical fitness nut. I like to run, swim and bike and I enjoy exercises that get me sweating. Not only do I feel good physically when I work out, but I also feel good emotionally and mentally.

One of the unfortunate disadvantages of living in the beautiful state of Florida is that there are few areas where one can bicycle and run safely. There are no sidewalks or bike paths in most neighborhoods and I happen to live in one of those.

I run on the streets near my home. On the extreme left side against traffic for safety reasons. A driver can see me running toward him and I can see a car approaching me ahead. Almost all drivers move away from the curb when they see me and I wave or nod to them to show my appreciation. When I see a car ahead and hear the engine of one coming from behind, I run off onto the shoulder of the road so that both cars can pass safely. So that I am safe as well.

One morning, while running on a quiet street, I saw a car approaching several hundred yards away. I glanced over my shoulder and noted no cars coming from behind me. I stayed on my path, expecting the driver to move to his left to allow me to continue running. Instead, the car came closer toward me without moving away from the curb. I saw that the driver, an elderly gentleman, was aiming for me and jumped off onto the grass some seconds before he might have hit me. His gesture indicated he was annoyed with me. One of those, "Get off the road," signals. "Roads," I was sure he was saying, "are for cars, not for runners."

"You old man," I thought, "why don't you go back up North? I bet you've never exercised a day in your life. I pay more taxes than you do for these roads. You inconsiderate, complete and total jerk."

I was angry and upset and I envisioned arguing with him about his lack of consideration, the threat to my life, my rights as a taxpayer, etc. I saw myself beating his car with my fists, shaking my index finger at his face. I must have spent ten minutes in a fit of relatively controlled rage while I continued running down the street.

I realized recently that I allow my thoughts—which I create—to affect my life negatively. I know now that while I spent ten minutes in rage and in anger over an inconsiderate driver, I was not "alive." It's clear to me as a runner and a biker that I can expect to experience these kinds of drivers; the elderly gentleman wasn't the first or last. Some of these drivers may be inconsiderate; but most, I think now, just lack awareness.

I continue to run and bike on the streets and I am more cautious. I had a choice. I could stop exercising completely or I could exercise and be prepared for an inappropriate action by some driver. When that happens now, I just let it go. This doesn't mean I don't get angry, upset or enraged. But, since I'm aware of what occurs, my outbursts have become shorter. Sometimes, I actually smile or laugh because I can picture what it did to me in the past.

It's perfectly acceptable to think and feel whatever we want to at any time. We need to be aware of the consequences of having thoughts and the feelings they produce. The consequence in my simple example of one driver was that I was not being alive.❀

Step Back

*W*hen we think negative thoughts or feel negative emotions such as self-pity, guilt, fear, blame, anger, sadness or disappointment, we need to step back, if only just a little. When we mentally remove ourselves from what is happening, we can ask, "Why am I thinking and feeling this way? Is this helping me or others in some way?"

We may see that there is no basis in for holding on to our negative thoughts or emotions. We may continue having them anyway or we may have them again with other people or in similar situations in the future. The more we practice stepping back—and sometimes stepping back a long way—and the more we ask the questions posed, the less time we'll spend on stepping back later.

This process is life-long. As soon as we think we've eliminated all negative thoughts and emotions, a new one assuredly pops up. This isn't good or bad. It's just the way it is. Step back, ask questions, become more aware, move on. When we step back far enough, we can even see ourselves going through the stepping back process.

On any given day, we're bombarded with negative thoughts. Thoughts that lead to negative emotions and negative behaviors. We can identify these thoughts and behaviors in ourselves. We can note when we are judgmental, prejudicial or blaming. The question we ask ourselves is not why others think or behave the way they do, but rather "Why do I?"

I know it's easier to point out the negatives in others "for their own good," but the only one I have total control over is me, the only one I can change is me. The only one you can change is you.◻

Choices and Responsibilities

Like an Oak Seed

*L*ike oak seeds, we grow from the inside out.

When we look at a mature oak tree, it's hard to imagine that, at one time, it was just a tiny seed. Within a single seed, there existed everything that the tree would eventually be. Its size and shape, its type and color were preprogrammed. We knew from the seed how it would turn out. Right?

Not exactly.

A lot of information about how a particular tree will grow can indeed be found in its seed. But, we would still know nothing about how much sunlight and wind would influence its growth. Nothing about the quantity of rain that would soak it, the temperature and other environmental influences that the tree might experience. While these outside influences won't change the tree's type, they will affect its growth.

Human beings, like oak seeds, are preprogrammed to a large degree. A lot of what each of us is today was determined genetically when a specific sperm united with a particular egg. And, like the oak tree, each of us is influenced by unpredictable environmental factors. Factors that will affect our physical and personal growth.

Unlike oak trees, we can move, make choices, experience outcomes and results and make more choices.

No matter what our specific genetic programming was and no matter what environmental factors have affected us, we need to know that growth happens to us from the inside out. It doesn't happen TO us. Growth happens FROM us.➤

Begin Choosing

We are born into life. It's waiting for us. We don't pick it. We just step into it on a day we don't choose. We step into who our parents are, whether we are first-borns or last-borns. We step into a part of the country, a part of the world We don't choose our appearance or the efficiency of our brains or other organs. But, soon, we realize that we have choices in who we will become and what we will do. And, when that occurs, we start building our own lives—a difficult task when we consider the limited number of days we are given to complete it. But, that's not important. What is important is to begin making those choices.

Paraphrased from a quote by Hugh Prather

Each of us is uniquely different. From the color of our skin to the amount of money in our wallets. From the plush comforts of our Manhattan penthouses to the dry barrenness of our Nicaraguan shacks.

But, all of us—each one of us—have something in common. And that is living life and making the choices it presents. It's a waste of our time and energy to expend both trying to figure out why we are who we are, why others are who they are.

We just must accept ourselves the way we are right now, right here. We must accept others the way they are, too.

We must choose acceptance and begin living this very moment.❖

Finding Happiness

*B*eing happy is everyone's ultimate goal, I think. We each have a different notion about what it is, how we will get it and how we will be when we have it. But, most of us agree that this is what we want from life—happiness.

What is happiness? It's an emotion. Something we feel inside of us. Most of us can make lists of people, situations, things and events that generate our happy feelings. We can talk about what happens when a person, situation, thing or event that brought us happy feelings is taken away from us. And how unhappy we feel then.

This is what tends to cause our lives to be a series of ups and downs. It's my opinion that these fluctuations also are the number one cause of our stress.

When persons, situations or events that brought us some happiness are not what we would like, our ability to be happy decreases. Most of us can find happiness some of the time, but wouldn't it be nice to feel happy more consistently? Wouldn't it be nice if we could avoid some of the valleys?

I believe we can do both by changing our perceptions and ideas about happiness.

If happiness is something inside of us—an emotion we generate—we need to take responsibility for it. For our own happiness.

No matter what is happening in our lives, each of us has a choice about how we process what is going on. The interpretations—thoughts—we process will, in turn, affect our emotions and our feelings.

We want to be happy. We want to feel good about ourselves. No matter what else is happening to us, we desire inner peace

155

and inner happiness. So much so that we are willing to do enormous deeds to try to be happy. To feel at peace.

We must realize that happiness and inner peace do not happen to us. That they are feelings that come FROM us. That we create our own happiness and our own inner peace through our own thoughts.

Being happy—having inner peace—begins with us. It starts inside each one of us. People and events will certainly have an affect on us. But, if we wait for "things" to happen to us to be happy, we will be expecting. We will be disappointed.

We may find happiness for a short time if we rely on people, events and situations to bring it to us, but as soon as something happens with those people events and situations, we will see that we were not happy inside. We will recognize that something external created temporary happiness.

People and events just cannot give us internal, lasting happiness. They cannot create our own personal sense of inner peace. We—only we—can create those feelings. No amount of money, no particular person—will do it for us over the long haul. We can have short-term happiness from external things, but ultimately that does not solve our wish for consistent happiness and inner peace.

Just as we know that our thoughts create our feelings and emotions, we know that we are capable of controlling our thoughts. Processing what happens to us in more productive ways. We know when we change our way of thinking, we can produce different feelings and emotions.

We must accept, then, that we are responsible for our happiness and our inner peace. That we—through our thoughts—are responsible for all of our feelings and our emotions.

While this may not be easy, it is freeing. We are no longer dependent on other people and outside events and situations for our temporary states of happiness. While "things" will still happen over which we have no control, we will know that it is we who create our thoughts. We who create our feelings and emotions.

It is we who will make us more consistently happy. Who will give us the greatest inner peace.◐

Happiness Prevails

$\mathcal{T}$o be happy, WE must choose to be happy.

Happiness is something we ARE. Not something we feel occasionally when everything seems to be going well.

It's as much a part of us as the color of our hair or the wrinkles around our eyes. Happiness is reflected in everything we do and in everything we say. It's a part of us.

When we are happy—when happiness feels a part of us— our ability to handle life and all its opportunities comes with inner strength and inner peace.

Death, disease, disappointment and tragedy continue to occur. They are part of life. And, some of us face more challenges in life than others of us do. But, everyone of us—to some degree or another—experiences life events that, if we had a choice, we would most decidedly avoid.

When something happens that we don't like, we may respond with anger, sadness, worry, fear or other emotions that are not synonymous with feeling happy. No matter what our reactions to events are, they are fine. They are okay.

When happiness becomes a part of our every fiber, though, the reactions we have to life events that we don't like—the events we would rather have avoided—are short-lived. They don't last long and they don't crumble us or our lives.

Happiness, you see, prevails.◻

157

Where Happiness Comes From

*O*ur happiness comes from experiencing love, acceptance and compassion. Without those feelings, real happiness is just not possible.

Each day, we are exposed to a wide range of challenging events and people. People who don't believe in the same things that we believe in. People who don't like what we like. People who do harmful things to other people.

If we have difficulty loving, accepting and being compassionate towards people who challenge us in one way or another, our opportunity to experience genuine happiness is limited. We must love, accept and have compassion for the world and for all of its inhabitants to be happy.

When we are exposed to events and people that are different from events and people we have been accustomed to, we can easily become confused, cynical, angry, bitter—certainly anything but happy. Because we are all different and because differences can produce some unpleasant feelings, we may tend to seek out people who are as much like us as we can possibly find. This may be why we go to certain churches, belong to specific clubs and organizations, have lunch and dinner with people whose beliefs and ideas are similar to our own.

Also, while some of us don't mind confrontation, most of us seem to mind it and, so, we like to be around people like ourselves because that tends to maximize agreement and to minimize or to avoid confrontation.

Like-minded individuals, we know, form groups to work toward like-minded causes. To be with others who share the same philosophies and goals. Some us may even spend our time with others who are like us just talking about people who are unlike us. We may even share with our friends a view that those who are different from us are "wrong" or even "bad" for being different from us.

I sometimes want to bet that more groups have probably been founded so that people can join together "against" other people's beliefs than have been founded so that people can join together to share their own beliefs.

That's not a manifestation of happiness. For happiness without love, acceptance and compassion for our differences is just not genuine. It is love, acceptance and compassion that brings happiness. When we have and display these, we are happy.

If any of my readers feel they are already as happy as they care to be and if they are not in agreement with what I'm saying about love, acceptance and compassion being the vehicle to happiness, I want them to know that I think their position is fine. That's their choice and I respect their right to make it. As I've written elsewhere, I believe that we all should be and do what works for each one of us.

What's in this book is just an expression of my own opinion and my own philosophy. Others will find their own path to happiness by traveling a different route, one that works wonders for them.

If life isn't working out as well for others as they would like, if the world just doesn't make sense to them, if they are not happy or if they're not happy enough, perhaps looking at my—or a different—approach might help.

I encourage exploring a variety of viewpoints for in them we may each find some truth and some satisfaction.

Do Others Enjoy Being Around Us?

For me, it's looking inside and discovering and developing love, acceptance and compassion. These are qualities I know we all possess.

I enjoy being around happy people. Probably all of us do. We're attracted to happy, energetic, fun-loving people because their feelings seem contagious. The more we are around them, the more we want to be with them.

We can all ask ourselves a simple question: do others like being around us? If we know they do, we are either happy people or, at the least, we know that others probably believe we are. This doesn't mean if we are loners or if we find ourselves alone a lot that we aren't happy. It's just something to think about.

Most of us probably don't like being around unhappy people. Except perhaps for those of us who are unhappy ourselves. Those of us who might feel good complaining. Those of us who are grumpy and depressed and seeking out those with like mind. If we have the choice, how many of us would go out of our way to be around depressing people? People who talk continuously about how unfair the world is?

When we are truly happy, it doesn't matter who we are around. Happy people energize each other. With unhappy individuals, our own happiness shines through. It has a beneficial effect on others. When we are happy, we can give and give and give and never lose anything.

When we allow others to affect our own happiness, we might question the authenticity of our happiness. For, I think, it should be fun to be around people who need our happiness. We ought to want to give them some of ours. It ought to feel like the win-win situation that it is.

The people we wouldn't choose to be around need us and our happiness the most. It's easy to be and stay happy when we're with other happy people. It's a test of our love, acceptance and compassion to be with unhappy people.

Just observe what you feel when you're around unhappy people.➤

Responding with Ability

*W*hen we were younger, responsibility had to do with making our beds, doing our homework, cutting the grass.

As we got older, it had to do with getting a good job, being a supportive spouse, taking care of our children.

All of these are tasks. Things to do. While tasks are a part of responsibility, there is another aspect to it.

What do we do when something happens to us over which we have no control? How do we handle situations we hadn't planned on but find ourselves smack in the middle of?

Responsibility is responding with ability to any person, place or thing. To any situation, circumstance or happening.

We are reacting and responding constantly. We respond physically or mentally. We take action with our bodies, which may include speaking, or we respond by producing thoughts. We usually respond using a combination of physical and mental actions.

Our entire existence, while we are awake, is a continuous series of reactions and responses. This is why responding with ability is so important.

Responsibility is not something we do part of the time; it's something we do all the time. We are what we think. We are what we do.

When we live our lives with responsibility—responding with ability to all life has to offer—we are empowered. We take complete and total control of our lives and no matter what happens to us, we take responsibility.

With responsibility, we don't blame someone or something for where we happen to be. Whether things are going smoothly or whether we're experiencing difficulty, responsibility means taking control of the situation. It means making necessary choices and taking appropriate actions.

We don't spend our precious time figuring out who to blame because we know that blaming gives someone or something else control over us. We know blaming gives away our power.

Life is full of challenges, obstacles and disappointments. When we respond with ability, people or situations do not control us. We maintain control of ourselves and our lives.

Taking responsibility for our lives is empowering and freeing. ❖

Responding with Unlimited Human Potential

*W*hen something "bad" happens to someone we know or love, it also happens to us because of our feelings for them. We know it's a waste of time and energy to search for something or someone to blame. We know that what's happened has already happened. That we cannot go back and change it.

We accept the situation and we respond with ability. We respond with love and compassion.

As much as we all would like to protect the people we love, we know that each of us has to experience life in our own way. This includes our children and our children's children and everyone else who inhabits our world. We don't want our children to suffer. We don't want "bad" things to happen to anyone who is unable to deal with a particular situation.

But we know we are only able to protect our loved ones for a short period of time. We know they will face obstacles, challenges and disappointments.

All we can do is give them love and compassion.

Whether someone we love is faced with an emotional or physical challenge, we can respond with love and compassion. We can provide the support they can use. We may feel like stepping in, feel like shouldering their responsibilities, but we know doing so would not allow them to grow.

Everyone must live his or her own life. Everyone must grow at a rate that is comfortable to them.

Allowing our children to experience life, to face challenges, obstacles and disappointments on their own, empowers them.

We are not turning our backs on them. We are providing pure love, acceptance and compassion. ☯

Empowerment and Freedom

I often suggest that when we change our thinking and/or our perceptions we become empowered, we become free.

What does this mean?

Being empowered and free means we take control of our lives. We understand that if we want to be happy—if we want inner peace if we want to feel good about ourselves, that we are the ones—the only ones who are in control of our becoming happy, enjoying inner peace, feeling good about ourselves.

To be sure, events and situations happen TO us—they always will. But when we are empowered and free, we are assured that, even when things happen to us, we can continue to make our own choices. We continue to be in charge of our decisions.

When we are empowered and free, we don't blame, condemn or criticize others for where we are or for what happens to us. We are in control. We take responsibility.

When we find ourselves afraid, depressed, angry or hating someone or something, we know we own these emotions and that having them is how we have chosen to process what is happening around us. We know we may continue to have the thoughts or feelings we are having but we know we can change them if we so choose. When we are empowered and free, we know everything—every single response—is up to us.

There will always be people and events in the world that upset or even sicken us. Either we will allow other people and external events to control our feelings and emotions or we will take control. With power and freedom, we accept that tragedies happen. We may not like them, but we accept them. We accept that there exists in our world some people who intentionally cause tragedies. With power and freedom, we simply choose our responses. We choose our feelings and emotions.

When we are empowered and free, no one can tell us what we SHOULD feel. We can choose to be angry or to hate or we can choose to feel love and compassion. Our feelings are in our control.

With power and freedom, we accept total responsibility for how we feel. We are entitled to blame certain events and certain people for certain situations, but, we know that when we do, we give up some of our power and some of our freedom. This is our choice to make.

When I've discussed some of these thoughts with friends, I have often been asked, "Don't you get mad and upset when you hear about kids being abused? Innocent kids?" Or, "Don't you get angry when an unsuspecting woman is raped?"

Yes, of course, I do. I get upset, mad and angry. But, let me explain this response from my perspective.

Firstly, I believe that no matter what I am feeling, I have chosen to feel it. It is my choice. If I am angry or upset with regard to abused kids or sexual assaults, I take responsibility for my responses. The person causing the abuse or rape isn't responsible for my responses. I am. Secondly, I know that what I choose to feel will not change what has already happened. No matter what I am feeling, I cannot change what has already occurred. Being upset, angry or hateful, I know, doesn't help anyone feel better. It doesn't help me feel better.

With power and freedom, we are choosing what we will feel. If being angry or upset works for us—if it enhances our lives and the lives of those around us we may wish to continue choosing those feelings. If being angry, upset and hateful doesn't add to our happiness, our inner peace, our good feelings about ourselves, then we may wish to change our responses. We may wish to take control of our feelings. With power and freedom, we know we can do that.

Sometimes, we do what we think we should do or what we think is the right thing to do. If someone does something "bad" (for example, performs a violent act against someone who is helpless), we may get mad and angry. We may experience rage.

We may seek to punish them. What will this accomplish? Nothing.

I am not saying we can't take action to prevent a violent act from happening again. I am saying that the action we decide to take ought not be based in feelings of hate, anger, rage and revenge. Our actions ought to be based in the love and compassion we have for other people, in the desire we have, for example, in assuring that other people are safer than they were before.

Let's look, for a moment, at events that occur that are simpler, less violent than abuse and rape.

What happens if we are walking behind someone who, while enjoying a hot dog, has decided to throw a wrapper on the sidewalk. Let's assume we intensely dislike littering. We have a lot of choices at our disposal; we know that we can make a choice in how we respond.

1. We can ignore the littering.

2. We can go nuts. We can rant and rave and become consumed thinking about how anyone could do such a rotten thing. We can even let this ruin our entire day.

3. We can calmly pick up the discarded wrapper and continue walking down the street.

4. We can pick up the paper, walk over to the man who dropped it and stick it in his face. We can deliver a lecture on how worthless and irresponsible he is.

5. We can pick up the paper and gently bring it to his attention, conveying hope that he will not litter again.

There is no right or wrong choice. The point is we choose. We decide which one of these choices adds to our happiness, to our sense of inner peace. We decide which choice enhances our lives and the lives of those around us.

The realization and the understanding that we make our own choices, to me, is the most exciting aspect of being empowered and having freedom. The realization that what we feel is based on what we choose to think and the knowing that we can change how we feel by changing what we think and what we choose to do or not do is an enormously powerful realization.□

The Universe

The Universe is Everything

$\mathcal{T}$he universe is everything. And it is one infinite universe.

If a group of families blasted off in a spaceship to find the end of the universe, they would never accomplish their goal. Generation after generation after generation would come and go, but the spaceship would continue on its journey. Without end. Without finding an end.

For if there were such a thing as an end to the universe, wouldn't we all still have to ask, "And, so, my friend, what comes after that? What comes after the end?"

If there is no end to the universe, can there ever have been a beginning? If someone theorizes a beginning point—any beginning point, wouldn't we have to ask, "What came before that? What was it precisely that came before the beginning?"

These questions can't be answered because there was no beginning to the universe and there can be no end.

What about God or unlimited human potential or spirit or consciousness or whatever the word with which we are comfortable? If the universe is everything, then God, a concept of the universe, is everything, too. He (or She or It) cannot be a separate entity. Not a separate concept. God encompasses everything that ever was, everything that will ever be. We are as much a part of the universe and everything as God or unlimited human potential is and God or unlimited human potential is a part of us, too.

As an analogy, if the universe is the ocean, then God or unlimited human potential is also the ocean. If we are sponges in the ocean, we are a part of the ocean and the ocean is a part of us. We cannot separate the ocean and its sponges; and we cannot separate ourselves from God or unlimited human potential.

So God or unlimited human potential is of us and we are of God or unlimited human potential.➤

The Universe is Perfect

$\mathcal{T}$he universe is perfect. It lacks nothing essential to the whole. God, which is the universe, is perfect; and we—you and I—another part of the universe and of God, are also perfect.

Does this mean that all of the choices we make and the behaviors we display are perfect?

Yes and no.

When we look at the big picture, we must answer yes. It has to be. But, when we look at the smaller picture—the isolated choices and behaviors—we might want to answer "no."

Let me explain. We are part of one perfection and, so being, our choices and behaviors are also a part of that one perfection.

If we were to isolate individual choices and behaviors, we might find them lacking in what is essential to the whole. We might find that what we choose and how we behave sometimes isn't perfect.

When a man decides to drink to the point of drunkenness and chooses, in his stupor, to drive a vehicle, his choice lacks what is essential to the whole. When a drunken driver hits and kills a child, we experience tragedy. This event, taken alone, does not enhance life. This isolated decision—like every decision—results in some consequence or another.

In this case, one man's decision and its subsequent consequence lacked what was essential to the whole. It was not perfect. To accept and to understand individual choices and events, we must look at their benefits to the whole. We must see the whole although it's not easy to do.

Let's look at the whole in this man's decision. What if this man, after killing this child, becomes rehabilitated and becomes directed toward giving lectures and workshops around the country to teach others to avoid drinking and driving? What if he becomes involved with Mothers Against Drunk Drivers (MADD) and starts a chapter in his city to increase awareness of the problem. How many people might be touched by him? How many of those touched by him might, in turn, spread the word and touch others?

One isolated choice with what appeared to be a non-life-enhancing consequence might lead to an infinite number of other choices, events and consequences. Some of those may be lacking. But, many will be life-enhancing. The whole, you see, is always perfect.

When we cannot see the perfection in the universe, we need to step back for a time. To become aware and open.

For a long time, we believed the earth was flat. We also believed the sun revolved around the earth. When we were able to step back far enough, we learned the earth was round; it revolved around the sun.

When we observe, read or listen to anything that causes us or others pain and sorrow, we must step back. Far enough to see the whole. Even when this is most difficult to do, we must remember: there is a whole; there is one universe which is God; God is perfect and the whole is perfect.

Even though the man who hit and killed a child turned his life around, will everyone involved in this incident be happy? No. Not at all. And, this may be said about any of our choices and about any of the events that proceed them. The father of the dead child could become so depressed that he might never function well as a husband or as a father to his remaining children. Would any of us consider that result to be perfect? Not by itself. For that result would cause much pain and sorrow for a great many people.

But, we know that an infinite number of other decisions and events will occur because of the father's choices. Some of those may cause additional pain and sorrow. Others will be perfect— lacking nothing essential to the whole.

Every choice—every decision—we make has a conse-quence. Each one of those consequences generates more choices and decisions. The circuitry and branching out of choices and decisions is infinite. It continues generation after generation.

There will never be an end because there was never a beginning. There is only ONE. The Whole.

I feel it's necessary to understand that there is a whole even though all of this might sound somewhat esoteric. It helps put individual people and events into perspective. If we can comprehend the whole, we can begin to accept people who do not have the whole in mind as they lead their lives.

Perhaps we find someone with whom we work obnoxious or offensive. Maybe it's someone we've read about in the newspaper—someone who has done "something" to someone else. While it's our right to be mad, angry, upset and stressed out with our co-workers, while it's our right to judge others for their crimes against humanity, what does this do for us, for them, for the victims of their behaviors?

Nothing. Absolutely nothing.

When we understand that there is a whole, we don't get stuck being angry, being stressed out or becoming judgmental. While these emotions and/or reactions are still elicited, they quickly vanish when we understand that all people and all events are part of the perfect whole.

I get mad, angry and upset, as I've confided elsewhere in this book. I find myself judging others, too. But, my emotions and reactions no longer consume me. I now am aware of what I'm feeling and I allow it to pass. The most difficult thing I'm handling now is to stop being mad, angry or upset with myself for feeling the feelings I know are unproductive. But, then, I know this is all part of the whole. These are emotions and reactions we need to experience so that we comprehend the whole and know that it should not be judged by its individual parts. ❖

The Preacher and I

I grew up believing that the world was not perfect. That people were sinners. That life was a struggle—a never-ending series of obstacles. Recently, I attended a fund-raising event for a local charity during which time I had an opportunity to talk with a Southern Baptist preacher.

This preacher expressed compassion for those who attended his church and, most especially, for those who were in need. I was calmed by his presence and felt the love he had for those around him. I shared with him my thoughts on the universe, the thoughts written in the pages preceding this one.

He agreed with me that the universe was everything and that God (or unlimited human potential) and the universe could not be separated. He also agreed that God (or unlimited human potential) was perfect.

I told him that if God—the universe and everything—is perfect and if we are as much a part of God as God is a part of us—and the universe—then we are perfect. That being said, I asked the preacher, then, to tell me why so many people tend to believe the world is not perfect. Why do people believe there are sinners? I wanted to know. Why do they believe that life is a struggle?

He smiled gently and told me I'd given him a lot to think about. But, also that I had forgotten a major detail. The preacher said, "God granted us free will—each of us has choices."

The preacher told me that free will—free choice—is the reason the world is in turmoil. The reason we have injustice and war.

I admired and respected him for his views and, time being limited, we agreed to get together in a few weeks to discuss further all this philosophizing.

When we again met, the preacher took from his pocket a small piece of paper on which he had scribbled some notes and arrows. He immediately began discussing his ideas with me. I knew he had done some serious thinking and was anxious to talk. He said:

You gave me a lot to think about the other day. While I'm not completely sure of what your point was, I wanted to express some of my feelings to you. I believe in God I believe God created everything and, therefore, that God is everything.

In order for me to believe in God, I must also believe that God has always been here. I must believe that God always was and ever will be. This means there is no beginning and no end.

I also believe in God's perfection. How could I not given what I just said? I agree with you on all of this. But not your belief that we human beings are perfect.

While this may have been God's intention, God did give us free will, the ability to make choices. This is what separates us from God.

God is perfect but we have made choices that have led to war, to poverty, to inequity. To the turmoil we are in. Don't get me wrong. We have also made wonderful choices that are full of love, compassion and are God-like in quality.

If all of us could be more God-like in our choices, there would be less turmoil and more peace. I believe that this is our purpose. As human beings created by God, we have been given the ability to make choices. The more all of us realizes this, the more decisions we will make that lead us towards peace and tranquillity. Towards God.

The preacher took off his glasses, rubbed his eyes, sat back in his chair and, clasping his hands, laid them on his lap. He smiled. It was my turn to respond:

I accept everything you said. My thoughts were similar to yours at one time and actually still are—except for a few different ideas.

The choices some individuals make are destructive. The behaviors some people display seem aimed at destroying other people. How can this be? I wonder.

If we were created by a loving, compassionate and forgiving God, why do people hurt other people? It is difficult to comprehend the whole by judging the parts.

We don't decide whether we like a painting by looking at each brushstroke. Each stroke by itself is unremarkable. Some could be judged rough. Some ugly. Some immature and amateurish.

But a whole painting—all the brushstrokes together— somehow create in the viewer a gambit of thoughts and emotions. Whether we feel happiness, sadness, passion, fear or confusion, we are, as viewers, touched by whole paintings—not individual strokes. This is my concept of the universe. This is my concept of God or unlimited human potential.

I see the oneness of it all I see the whole of the universe, of God, of perfection. I acknowledge the parts, but I trust the whole.

Since God is everything and God is perfection, then everything is perfection. Some parts of the whole are rough. They're ugly. They're immature. There is prejudice, hate, poverty and war. But, I sleep soundly acknowledging and accepting the parts as I view the whole. This is peaceful. To look at the oneness of the universe and trust in its perfection.

This is our fundamental difference. We agree that God is everything and that God is perfect. You feel that free will and the ability to make choices somehow separates us from God. But, if God is everything, then how can we be separate from God? I believe we cannot. If God is everything, then individual thought and choice are as much a part of God as are the blue sky and the solar system

Our thoughts, our choices, our behaviors—whether we choose to judge them or not—are part of the whole, part of the perfection. All parts are necessary. All parts are essential

The preacher and I enjoyed interacting. We enjoyed talking, sharing and accepting. I was not trying to convince him to change his way of looking at our perfection. He was not trying to convince me to change my way of looking at it. There is no right and no wrong. There just is. I had a wonderful time with him. He did not judge, but rather just let me be. He listened, accepted and loved. I learned much from a most compassionate man and I thank him for that. ❧

Trust in the Whole

I feel tested every day. Whether it's by someone with whom I come into contact or by someone I read about in the newspaper or see on television. There are displays of behavior, events that take place and attitudes I witness that I don't like.

There are people starving in the streets. Homeless and poverty-stricken children. There are people being abused, raped and murdered. Countries all around the world in turmoil.

It's not easy to think about perfection with all this happening around us. It almost seems selfish.

It's much easier to talk about perfection when everything is going well. I ask myself almost daily what it would be like if I lived in South Africa. Or if I had been born black. What if my wife were raped? What if my child had a life-threatening disease?

While it's easy to accept the notion of perfection of the whole when things are going well, it is when life is going poorly for us that the idea is most useful. Trusting in the whole is not only helpful. It's essential.

When we read of people's struggles in this or other countries—when we hear that some are lashing out against us in the United States—we must step back. Step back far enough to see the whole. To trust the perfection of the whole. Or else, each day will surely be a struggle.

We don't need to turn off our radios or to stop watching the evening news. The answer is within all of us.

We must trust in the big picture. Trust in the whole. Love, accept and be compassionate with ourselves, with others, with the world.☯

Letting Go of the Past; Living in the Moment

Accept the Past—
Now Let it Go

*C*hanging ourselves isn't easy. We can't take a specific behavior or attitude we've had for a long time and casually alter it. We can't just simply decide we want to change and then will it to happen. We may wish we could, but it isn't so simple a task.

I'm not talking about driving a new route to work or reading the newspaper in the evening instead of the morning.

I'm talking about the behaviors and attitudes we have that are deep-rooted. They've developed over a long period of time. Behaviors and attitudes we don't like in ourselves are as difficult to change as the ones we do like. I think this is because, for the most part, we have to know why we are the way we are in order to change. If we don't understand at least a part of why we are the way we are, I think that change is impossible.

When we can identify some of the reasons—the real reasons—why we are the way we are, then change is not only possible. It is easy, immediate and permanent.

WORRY

Many of us spend our present time worrying about what might or might not happen. We worry about what has already happened. Worrying is so common that we consider it a normal human function. Intellectually, though, we know worrying doesn't do us any good. That it affects us negatively. That we don't want to worry. That we don't like worrying. Yet, most of us continue to worry. When asked why we worry, we probably say, "Because I can't help it. It's just the way I am."

187

And, we continue worrying. About health, money, relationships, the environment, world peace, global warming, weather, exams, school, work and on and on. Why?

FEAR

We spend much of our time being afraid. Fearing things and events we know we shouldn't fear. Some of us, for example, are afraid to fly. We may say, "It's because we have no control." We may say that we're safer when we're driving a car because we're in control. But, when we're reminded that we have no control over other drivers on the road or that the statistics tell us otherwise, we concede that flying may be safer than driving. This doesn't stop us from being afraid. We may not want to be; we may not like to be. But, the fear of flying isn't something we can just change. There is a reason for it that is deep-rooted. And, until it's revealed to us, we will not be able to change it.

Fear is well-accepted in our society. Some say it's normal. Is it?

Fear is one of our most primitive emotions. It's part of the fight or flight phenomenon, integral to our survival. Fear is a present-time kind of emotion, one that helps us take appropriate actions when confronted with life-threatening situations. But, when we look at the list of fears most people have, we see that almost all of them have nothing to do with life or death.

We are afraid of small spaces, heights, elevators, the outdoors, the unknown, public speaking, failure, success, dogs, love and so on. None has to do with our survival.

Some of us experience fear each and every day of our lives. Like worry, we know, intellectually, that being afraid doesn't help us. That we don't like and don't want it. But, we are afraid. Why?

GUILT

Guilt is also well-accepted in our society. "Our parents," some of us say, "are always trying to make us feel guilty." Our friends, co-workers and religious leaders elicit guilt in us. Yes, we know, no one can "make" us feel anything. That only we can do that to ourselves. But, when we look at how we're brought up, at how society and religion motivate us to conform, we know it's easy for us to feel guilty about a myriad of our behaviors and thoughts. This is not an excuse. It is a fact.

Most of us don't like feeling guilty. We know that it changes nothing. That it serves no purpose. But, getting rid of it isn't easy. Why do we feel guilty about anything and everything? Why do we motivate our kids, partners and friends with guilt?

SELF-ESTEEM

How do we feel about ourselves?

Self-esteem is an issue for many of us, even those of us who know intellectually that we ought to feel good about who we are. We can make lists of our positive and negative traits, our accomplishments and good deeds. And, in reviewing them, we can see the proof of why we ought to feel good about ourselves.

But, it doesn't work to change our low self-esteem because the issue of self-esteem is no common sense exercise. Why?

HAPPINESS

No one can make us happy. No one can make us anything at all. Our partners, families, friends and our jobs are part of our lives, but none can make us happy. Being happy is an emotion that is totally in our control. While events do happen around us, we are still in control of our own happiness.

If this is true and we want to be happy, why aren't we?

Much of what we are is subconscious. Consciously, we often have no idea why we are the way we are.

I read books written by and listen to audio tapes recorded by Wayne Dyer. From his materials, I've learned much that has influenced my thinking and my view of life. But, he says that if we want to change, we ought to JUST DO IT. I disagree. I don't think change works that way.

So much of what we are is beyond our reach, beyond our conscious awareness. No matter how much we want to change. I don't think it can take place until we can identify some of the reasons we are the way we are. This is why we do what we do. When we understand this, we can change.

We, as a society, are more enlightened now than we've ever been in terms of identifying past events that have influenced our personalities. Some of the events in our histories are subtle; others quite dramatic. The particulars of the events that have taken place in our lives—whether they are small or large—are not important at this time. We must just identify and accept that these events have occurred.

Psychotherapists, psychoanalysts, psychiatrists, psychologists and other mental health professionals approach identifying our histories in various ways. Some professionals and some methods are more effective than others.

What's important is what we do with this information. Do we want to change? Or, do we want to go on a fact-finding mission so that we can lay blame for the events from our past?

Some of us identify past events to discover why we are the way we are and then, knowing this, fault others for it. We continue feeling miserable about ourselves and them and we do nothing to produce beneficial change.

I know that our parents take a lot of heat for "messing us up." It's probably correct to assume they caused some of our problems. They are our major teachers so they had the greatest effect on us—both for the good and for the bad.

But, so what?

Our parents did the very best that they could do with their own levels of awareness. Period.

We can't change what's already happened. We can't change what our parents did or did not do to us or for us. We can't change what happened to them that made them who they were or are to us. If we dwell on this, we get stuck in the past.

We Can Only Change Ourselves

While the past needs to be examined—even dissected—it's only necessary to do so if we are interested in now and in the future. What we do today has a direct influence on our future and what we will become. What our parents did or didn't do in the past won't help us in the present or in the future. If we really want change so that we may better enjoy now and the future, that is possible.

If we want to be a positive influence on our children or on others, this is possible. We must use our knowledge of why we are the way we are as tool for change. Not judge the past. Not be angry with the past. Not blame the past or others. Just accept it.

We cannot change the past, but we can change ourselves by using the past to change the present. The present will lead us to a future that is designed and choreographed by us.

A wonderful, peaceful and happy future.❐

Learn From the Past— Now Let it Go

J've never been fond of doing yard work. I do like looking at a manicured landscape, but I don't like doing what's required to make it so. I don't derive satisfaction from working around the house, though I know many people who do. Am I lazy? I don't think so because I don't mind hard work. I've done hard work during my life. I just know that when it comes to yardwork, I'd prefer being counted out.

When I was a youngster and my brother and two sisters had moved away from home, I inherited responsibility for the yard. I did as little as I possibly could with regard to trimming, weeding and edging. But, I was required to mow. Most of the time, I cut the lawn without being reminded. But, there were occasions when I just wasn't motivated. That was when my mother stepped in.

She'd remind me several times before she used her particular motivating techniques. She didn't threaten me by taking away privileges or by grounding me or by not letting me use the car. My mother used guilt.

I'd be watching "The Three Stooges" or a "Tarzan" movie on TV, for example, and she would remind me that the lawn needed cutting. I'd tell her I would do it right after one of these shows was over and, I think, I really would have. But, within a few minutes, I'd hear the lawn mower running and, there behind it, I'd find my mother pushing it.

I'd get mad. I'd scream at the top of my lungs and then I would, with great resentment, take over the task of mowing. I did what my mom wanted, but I certainly didn't like it. She motivated me, but I resented it. While my relationship with my mother is as good as anybody's—and while we both have looked back on these incidences and laughed at them—I know there's something to this guilt thing that has kept my lawn mowing memories alive for me for more than 25 years.

I remember the end of the summer when I was 18 years old. My father, mother and brother drove me to Kansas City, to the home of my cousin. Both he and I had accepted football scholarships to the University of Kansas. I remember my excitement. It overshadowed whatever it was my mother was going through. I was her youngest and last child at home and I was leaving the nest for school. A location more than 1200 miles from our home.

Looking back now, I can almost understand her sadness and her feelings of emptiness at the prospect of my going. I probably made it a lot worse for her because I ignored her and my father and brother. I didn't do this on purpose. I was just so excited about going away, attending college, being with my cousin and a third guy who would become our roommate that nothing else entered my mind.

I drove over to the university with my cousin and new friend, while my family followed behind us. I didn't think about hurting anyone's feelings and I didn't intentionally ignore them.

The night before my family would leave me to drive back to Wisconsin, we had dinner at my cousin's home in Kansas City. My mother called me aside for a private talk. One I'll never forget.

"It doesn't seem like you love us, John," she said. I was dumbfounded. She relayed her hurt feelings and I relayed mine. While she realized she may have overreacted, I felt tremendous guilt from her words. I was frustrated and angry at her. She knew I loved them, I thought, so why did she, why would she, say this?

I didn't show my resentment, but I was very upset. I just could not believe she said what she had to me. How could she? I repeated many times in my head.

As the fall slipped away, I remembered that event and, although I was no longer as upset with it as I had been initially, I chose not to go home for Thanksgiving break because of it. It may have been my way of getting back at my mother. My holiday absence hurt her and, of course, restimulated my feelings of guilt.

My mother and I have discussed this incident. She doesn't remember it. I consider it a major event in my life and still recall it as if it happened yesterday. Guilt is powerful.

And, hindsight is almost always 20-20.

I have told my mother on several occasions that my childhood experience—the way she brought me up—was wonderful. I know it's easy to look back and find fault and blame. This is not my message at all.

These two incidences are a part of my life experience and contribute to who I am today. I have chosen to relay these isolated events for two reasons. One is to acknowledge that guilt is definitely a motivator. It works, but it causes resentment,

> ***Hindsight is almost always 20-20***

bitterness and a breakdown in any relationship. Secondly, all of us can look back and find people in our past who seemed to try to make us feel badly. We can continue to look back with resentment and bitterness toward them or we can begin looking back with acceptance.

Whether it's our parents, teachers, brothers or sisters, our ministers, priests or rabbis, everyone around us was doing the very best that they could do based on their levels of awareness at those times.

When we continue feeling resentment and bitterness, when we still blame and find fault, those people and those events have a real hold on us. We allow them to continue controlling us. This is limiting.

When we can accept past events simply as experiences in our lives, we are empowered. Accepting those events and the people who participated in them is freeing and limitless.

It has a direct influence on our present relationships as well. If we stay limited about our past experiences—if we stay stuck in how we may have felt then we will practice guilt, resentment, bitterness and blame in our present relationships.➤

All We Have is Now

*T*o be completely alive may be an impossible task, but it's still one for which we can strive. To be totally alive, we must live in the moment. Neither in the past nor in the future.

When we live in the present moment, there are many rewards. There is, for example, no blame, worry, fear, anger, prejudice, judgment, guilt, revenge, sadness, depression, grief, competition, hatred, self-pity or feelings of worthlessness or hopelessness.

While we do want to live in the moment, our goal would not suggest forgetting the past or ignoring the future. We would just want to live each day more fully and more completely. To be alive.

This doesn't mean we won't grieve over the loss of a loved one or that we won't look forward to a joyous future family gathering. It doesn't mean we won't recall elements of our past with great fondness.

We're human beings and we have thoughts and they generate emotions. We can grieve, look ahead and reminisce and still be alive today.

It's just that the more we grieve, anticipate or reminisce, the less of today we have. This isn't good or bad. It's just something to think about—to be aware.

My dad passed away in the fall of 1979. I can look back to the days when he was alive and remember the wonderful times we had together. For a short period of time, while I reminisce about him, I am not living in the present moment. This is okay. But, when reminiscing about the past becomes obsessive, it may affect our aliveness today.

Our thoughts do drift to the past and that may produce feelings of happiness or sadness, joy or terror. We go to work in the morning thinking about the day's end. We sit at our desks on Mondays thinking about Friday night. We spend time in the past and in the future, but, we know, the present moment is all there really is.

We need to be aware of our thoughts, to notice if we are thinking about the past or the future. While we know this is okay and normal, we know, too, that we must let go of the past and the future to remain alive in the present moment.

All we have is now. ❖

Strawberries

I have heard this old Zen tale many times from various people who each seemed to tell it differently. I've changed the story myself just a bit—to convey something I think has been important for me to learn.

A wise farmer lived among the woods with his wife and three children. I don't know why he was considered wise. He just was. He loved being a farmer, loved working the fields and touching the Earth. He felt good plowing land, planting seeds and watching, eventually, his crops grow and mature. Not only did he feel happy about himself and how he was able to provide for his family, but he also enjoyed taking his surplus into town where he could share the fruits of his labors with others who appreciated what he grew.

Early one morning, while his wife was preparing breakfast, she asked the farmer to fetch some fresh cold water from their stream. The children, who normally did this task, were asleep and their mother did not want to wake them. He was reading a book he enjoyed, but, put it down quickly since he was more than happy to help her.

Walking down to the stream, the farmer felt the cool morning air on his face. He took in the vast land expanse and the sun rising on the horizon. He breathed in the fresh smelling air and listened as the birds chirped their morning songs.

When he reached the stream, the farmer saw that the water was crystal clear and appealing. Before filling his container with it, the farmer cupped his hand and drank from the stream. The water was sweet and cold and he felt refreshed as he sipped it.

As he began filling a porcelain container with water from the stream, the farmer heard an ominous growl behind him. He turned to find two big bears approaching. The farmer ran, crossing over the stream with the bears in pursuit. He came upon a well-worn dirt path unobstructed by trees or shrubs. As he ran down it, he found himself at a vaguely familiar spot where the path split in two. He recalled being here before and remembered that one path led to a tiny cave which would assure him safety. The cave's opening, he recalled, was just large enough for his medium-size frame—not big enough for either of the bears who were after him.

Try as he might, the farmer couldn't remember which path went where and so he chose the one on his left. Running at full speed down that path, he suddenly realized he had taken the one that would not lead him to the cave. He continued to run because the bears were right behind him. Feeling his chest pounding, the farmer was aware he would not be able to run at his present speed for very long.

At that point, he saw the path ending and found himself on the edge of cliff. He stopped abruptly, looked down and spotted a long winding vine leading from the cliff's perch to the bottom of a rocky valley some 50 feet below. The vine, he thought, was his chance to escape from the bears.

As he began climbing down the vine, the farmer glanced down to see another bear below him. This one, perched on his hind legs and growling louder than the other two bears, stared menacingly at him. The farmer changed directions and, tightly grasping the vine, he climbed back up. When he looked upward, he saw the other two bears waiting for him at the cliff's edge.

Clutching the vine tightly with both hands, the farmer positioned himself halfway between the two hungry bears above and the one below. When he glanced upward, he noticed two mice making breakfast of the vine he was grasping. It was only a small matter of time before they would eat through his lifeline, he was thinking, when he noticed something off to his right. It was the reddest, juiciest-looking strawberry he had ever seen. Holding onto the vine with his left hand, he reached out with his right and yanked the fruit from its stem. It was huge, ripe and sweet-looking. Glistening with dew, the strawberry was mouth-wateringly luscious. The farmer closed his eyes and slowly opened his mouth. As his teeth pierced its bright red skin, the strawberry's sweet juice squirted into his mouth. He did not chew rapidly, did not devour the strawberry in a single bite. The farmer chose to eat it slowly, to fully experience the best strawberry he had ever tasted.

This is the end of the story.

A wise, kind and gentle farmer had eliminated all thought from his mind. Just moments before he would, with certainty, fall to his death from the top of a cliff, he had enjoyed the simple taste of a well-grown strawberry. Holding tightly onto a vine, caught between two bears above and one below him, the farmer was happy. We ask how is this possible?.

This farmer's thoughts were not on his past. Not on his future. His thoughts were in the moment. And, in that precise time, he found an unusually succulent strawberry which he was able to enjoy fully.☯

The Farmer

*S*uppose the farmer in the story about the strawberry was not wise. What could he have been doing instead of living in the moment?

We know he was in an unfavorable position. Indeed, he was about to die. He could have been thinking about what got him in this predicament in the first place. Was it his sleeping children? His wife, who could not prepare the morning meal without that water? Was it he? He picked the wrong path, didn't he? If he had picked the path to the cave, he could have sat in it, waited until the bears grew tired and went on their way and, then, he could have gone safely home. But, he didn't do that. No, no, no. He chose the wrong path. And, now, he was holding on to an almost chewed-through vine waiting for death.

What will his wife do without him? His kids? He will not grow old alongside the woman he loves. He won't see his children grow up, marry, have children of their own. His wife will probably find another man. His kids will forget him. When the mice get through eating the vine, he will fall into the arms of the bear waiting below. Just imagine what that bear will do to him. Tear him apart, for sure. He will die in excruciating pain.

The farmer could have had those or similar thoughts. But, he did not. He was not consumed with what happened or what might happen. He was in the moment and that moment contained one gorgeous-looking, sweet-tasting strawberry.

There was nothing he could do about what had already transpired. Nothing he could do about what would happen in the next few minutes or next ten years.

This isn't to say that the farmer gave up. Rather, that he chose to accept the moment he was in and live it fully.

The strawberry story is obviously a piece of fiction. But, consider this. Don't we know lots of people who live their lives like the second scenario? Don't people we know blame others for their predicaments? Don't people blame themselves? Don't people worry about what might happen? About things that may never happen? Some people live with guilt. They are consumed thinking about what they should or should not have done. Feeling guilty about events they absolutely could not control.

When we are living life with guilt, worry and/or blame, we are living life in either of two states—in the past or in the future. Noted author Wayne Dyer has said, "It's impossible to live in the past or to live in the future. What you are doing is living now, thinking about the past or the future."

If we live life thinking about the past or the future, we can't expect to enjoy now. And now is all we have. We do not have the past. We do not have the future. All we have is the present. If we use the present to dwell on the past or worry about what lies ahead, we will have no now.

If we have no now, this experience called life does not exist.◻

Final Thoughts

Sweet Potatoes

*J*apanese scientists conducted an experiment using monkeys who were living in their natural habitat, a group of tiny islands far from civilization.

The researchers brought in a large supply of sweet potatoes, which the monkeys ate freely. On one island, it was observed, a young female monkey began washing her sweet potatoes before eating them. Soon, her playmates began washing their potatoes before eating them, too. Over time, more and more monkeys made it their practice to wash the sweet potatoes before putting them in their mouths.

One day, the most amazing event happened. All the monkeys on the island washed their sweet potatoes before eating them. Even those monkeys living on the opposite side of the island—monkeys who had never seen another monkey perform the task. But, far and away the most remarkable observation the scientists recorded was that on that very same day, all the monkeys on all the other islands began washing their sweet potatoes before eating them, too. Before that day, on most of the islands, not one of the monkeys had done this task. On this day and for all the days observed thereafter, each one of them did.

This incident has opened the door to greater experimentation and observation, most of it directed at understanding humans. Scientists have a theory to corroborate. Is it possible that when enough people think about something—any one thing—that other people in other places begin thinking about it, too.

When a person's thoughts are consumed with a particular subject, we notice that other people become concentrated on it, too. Even with no physical contact among them, more and more people seem to become consumed with the same thoughts.

This is not the same as what is referred to as the "snowball" effect, when one person tells another who tells two others who relay it to four others, etc.

With a maximum number of people thinking about unlimited human potential, perhaps we will see a soaring of love, acceptance and compassion.➤

I Change, You Change,
We All Change

I choose to believe that all of us are inherently good. I choose to believe we are all on the rim of the wheel. That we are all equal in value as human beings. That within all of us is an inner core of beauty. A core full of love, acceptance and compassion.

If this is true, we may ask why does our world sometimes seem full of hate, prejudice, injustice, war, hunger and homelessness? Why is it that some people purposely hurt others? Why are our children abused? Why are the old forgotten?

The answer is simple. We allow our behaviors, our thoughts, our decisions and our actions to take place—or to be motivated—by hate, fear, prejudice, blame, guilt and judgment rather than by love, acceptance and compassion.

If we allow love, acceptance and compassion to guide our thoughts and hence our behavior, we cannot possibly—we will not—live in an unjust world.

To Change the World,
We Must First Change Ourselves.

To change the world, we must first change ourselves. But, change is not our goal. When our thoughts and behaviors come from within—are guided by love, acceptance and compassion—the world may or may not change. But, our view of the world surely will.❖

My Posters

*I*n my office at home, two framed posters hang from a wall. They were written by Jan Michelsen.

One is titled TRUST LIFE; the other BE ALIVE. Both posters are bright, brilliant and bold. Each one has its own set of short phrases and sentences to go with its title. Many express profound wisdom in simple words.

In the last decade, a number of books have been written on these topics, with authors choosing their own ways to communicate what they feel about trusting life and being alive. No two are alike. This is what is written on my posters:

BE ALIVE

Think freely.

Practice patience.

Smile often.

Savor special moments.

Make new friends.

Rediscover old ones.

Tell those you love that you do.

Feel deeply.

Forget trouble.

Forgive an enemy.

Pick some daisies.

Share them.

Keep a promise.

Look for rainbows.

Gaze at stars.

See beauty everywhere.

Work hard.

Be wise.

Try to understand.

Take time for people.

Make time for yourself.

Laugh hardily.

Spread joy.

Take a chance.

Reach out.

Let someone in.

Try something new.

Slow down.

Be soft sometimes.

Celebrate life.

Believe in yourself.

Trust others.

See a sunrise.

Listen to rain.

Reminisce.

Cry when you need to.

Hope.

Grow.

Be crazy.

Count your blessings.

Observe miracles.

Make them happen.

Discard worry.

Give.

Give in.

Trust enough to take.

Trust life.

Have faith.

Enjoy.

Comfort a friend.

Have good ideas.

Learn.

Make some mistakes.

Learn from them.

Explore the unknown.

Hug a kid.

TRUST LIFE

Explore your heart.

Reach out.

Aim high.

Live fully.

Discard hate.

Release fear.

Let go of guilt.

Take a break.

Unwind.

Embark on adventure.

Let yourself go.

Cherish your creations.

Appreciate your uniqueness.

Accept your humanness.

Envision excellence.

Exude enthusiasm.

Be inspired.

Inspire others.

Recognize inner beauty.

Draw on inner strength.

Look inside your soul.

Embrace peace.

Seek truth.

Spread joy.

Launch new ideas.

Think big.

Accept challenges.

Expect the best.

Be your best.

Find happiness.

Be kind to others.

Be good to yourself.

Know that you are loved.

Take risks.

Learn from failure.

Enjoy success.

Share your gifts.

Love openly.

Do a good deed.

Have compassion.

Cry real tears.

Be humble.

Forgive.

Hug away a hurt.

Mend a broken heart.

Transcend self doubt

Abandon worry.

Ask for help.

Accept the kindness.

Call a friend.

Invite pleasure.

Live simply.

Smile frequently.

Treasure golden moments.

Luxury simple pleasures.

Wish upon a star.

As you've probably guessed, the words on these posters are interchangeable. They work together because to be alive, you must trust life. To trust life, you must be alive.

What if we all memorized the lists? What if we taught our children to memorize them, too? What if we accepted the wisdom in these phrases and discussed what they mean to each of us?

We received an education from our parents. As parents, we pass on much to our children. Wouldn't it be nice to pass on to others the simple, but essential, wisdom in these phrases? Wouldn't we benefit from this now and in the future?

This is probably not realistic. But, what a wonderful dream. ❧

Bibliography

Anthony, Robert. *50 Ideas That Can Change Your Life!* Berkley, 1982.

Bach, Richard. *Illusions.* Dell Publishing, 1977.

Benson, Herbert. *Your Maximum Mind.* Random House, Inc., 1987.

Berman, Phillip L. *The Courage of Conviction.* Dodd, Mead & Company, Inc., 1985.

Burnham, Sophy. *A Book of Angels.* Ballantine Books, 1990.

Burnham, Sophy. *Angel Letters.* Ballantine Books, 1991.

Buscaglia, Leo. *Love.* Ballantine Books, 1972.

Chopra, Deepak. *Perfect Health.* Harmony Books, 1991.

Cousins, Norman. *Head First.* Penguin Group, 1989.

Covey, Stephen. *The 7 Habits of Highly Effective People.* Fireside, 1989.

Dewey, Barbara. *As You Believe.* Bartholomew Books, 1985, 1989.

Dyer, Wayne. *Gifts From Eykis.* Pocket Books, 1983.

Dyer, Wayne. *The Sky's the Limit.* Pocket Books, 1980.

Dyer, Wayne W. *Your Erroenous Zones.* Avon Books, 1976.

Gawain, Shakti. *Creative Visualization.* Whatever Publishing, Inc., 1978.

Gibran, Kahlil. *The Prophet.* Alfred A. Knopf, 1923.

Goldman, Karen. *The Angel Book.* Simon & Schuster, 1988, 1992.

Hay, Louise L. *The Power is Within You.* Hay House, Inc., 1991.

Holmes, Ernest. *The Science of Mind.* G. P. Putnam's Sons, 1938.

Kübler-Ross, Elisabeth. *On Death and Dying.* Macmillan Publishing Co., Inc., 1969.

Kushner, Harold S. *When Bad Things Happen to Good People.* Avon Books, 1981.

Maslow, Abraham H. *Toward a Psychology of Being.* Van Nostrand Reinhold, 1968.

Millman, Dan. *No Ordinary Moments.* H.J. Kramer, Inc., 1992.

Millman, Dan. *Way of the Peaceful Warrior.* H.J. Kramer, Inc., 1980, 1984.

Peale, Norman Vincent. *Stay Alive All Your Life.* Ballantine Books, 1957.

Peale, Norman Vincent. *You Can if You Think You Can.* Prentice Hall Press, 1974.

Robbins, Anthony. *Unlimited Power.* Ballantine Books, 1986.

Robbins, John & Mortifee, Ann. *In Search of Balance.* H.J. Kramer, Inc., 1991.

Siegel, Bernie S. *Peace, Love & Healing.* Harper & Row, Inc., 1989.

Silverstein, Shel. *The Giving Tree.* Evil Eye Music, Inc., 1964.

Williamson, Marianne. *A Return to Love*. HarperCollins Publishers, Inc., 1993.

Williamson, Marianne. *A Woman's Worth*. Random House, Inc., 1993.

Index

About the Author

A physician with a great interest in how the mind can work to help us lead healthier, more productive lives, John Morgan has been exploring the views from other people's desks for several years. An avid reader, listener and observer, he has attended numerous seminars and lectures on health, happiness and success. An avid participator in life, he has studied hypnotherapy and enjoyed firewalking.

A triathlete, John Morgan excelled in sports as a youngster, garnering a yet-unbroken high school shot-put record and becoming an All-State football player. He was the recipient of a full athletic scholarship to the University of Kansas where he started for three years and was elected football team captain in his senior year. He played in the Liberty Bowl, Sun Bowl and, for a short time, with the New York Jets.

Morgan coached at the University of Kansas where he received a master's degree in education with an emphasis on health and kinesiology.

An educator, Morgan taught science and became the youngest head football coach in Pinellas County, Florida, before deciding to return to academics for a doctorate degree in chiropractic. He graduated *cum laude*.

A successful entrepreneur with a thriving practice in Florida, Dr. Morgan spends most of his free time writing and teaching techniques for fulfilling unlimited human potential.